"Near The Knuckle Chuckle"

**Other books available from the
Daily Record and Sunday Mail collection:**

The Billy Sloan Rock and Pop Quiz Book

The Jim Traynor/Hugh Keevins Sports Quiz Book

The 2002 Prize Crossword Book

Joe Punter At The Races

You Are My Larsson by Mark Guidi and Ewing Grahame

The Martin O'Neill Story by Anna Smith and David McCarthy

**Videos available from the
Daily Record and Sunday Mail collection:**

LUBO - A Gift From God

Tam Cowan's JOKE BOOK

Daily Record

"Near The Knuckle Chuckle"

sunday mail

First published 2001
by the Scottish Daily Record and Sunday Mail Ltd

ISBN 0-9513471-5-2

Copyright © Daily Record and Sunday Mail Ltd 2001

British Library Cataloguing in Publishing Data:
A catalogue record for this book is available
from the British Library.

Printed and bound in Great Britain

AS a youngster Tam Cowan was a regular in his school football team and a regional verse-speaking champion. But it was when he reached his late teens that Tam discovered his true talents - writing jokes and eating curries. After contributing material to Little and Large, Roy Hudd and Naked Video, Tam began writing about his favourite sport - football. His success in print led to him presenting the football fanzine show "Off The Ball" on Radio Scotland. Today Tam's popular football column appears twice a week in the Daily Record. He has also transferred his unique brand of football humour to the small screen with his "Offside" programme on BBC1 Scotland. Tam's previous TV outings include "Taxi For Cowan" - a comedy travelogue around Scotland.

In tandem to his media career, Tam has tirelessly kept eating and contributes a weekly restaurant review column to the Daily Record's Saturday Magazine. When not working, Tam relaxes by watching Motherwell FC, listening to Englebert Humperdink, and making roasted cheese on the grill. Tam's favourite holiday destinations are Las Vegas and Rothesay.

Booze & Banter

Pubs are full of humour... some of it is even intentional. But let's be honest, after a few bevvies you'll laugh at anything.

A MAN walks into the pub with an alligator on a lead. He tells the punters present that, for a round of drinks from everyone there, he will insert his manhood into the alligator's mouth and remove it unscathed. All the regulars accept the dare and each puts up a drink.

The man walks up to the alligator, takes his knob out of his pants and puts into the alligator's mouth. He then grabs a beer bottle and smashes it over the alligator's head. The alligator immediately opens its mouth and the man pulls out unscathed. The crowd is left in awe.

The man then says: "If there is anyone here who is willing do the same thing, I will give them £500."

From the back of the bar a woman stands up and says: "I'll do it, if you promise not to smash the beer bottle over my head!"

A WOMAN walks into a pub that has a sign saying: "Men Only."
"Sorry love," says the barman. "We only serve men in this place."
"That's OK," she says. "I'll take two of them."

ONE night a man was getting very drunk in a pub. He staggered back to go to the toilet, whipping it out as he went in the door. However, he had wandered into the Ladies by mistake, surprising a woman sitting on the toilet.

"This is for women," she screamed.

The drunk waved his dick at her and said: "Well, so is this!"

10

A MAN walks into a pub with a giraffe and they proceed to get blitzed. The giraffe drinks so much it passes out on the floor. The man gets up and heads for the door to leave when the publican yells: "Hey! You can't leave that lyin' there!"

The drunk replies: "That's not a lion! It's a giraffe."

GUY walks into a pub. The barman looks him up and down and says: "Hey, you've got a steering wheel on your knob."

The man replies: "Aye, it's driving me nuts!"

A NAGGING wife was complaining about her husband spending all his time at the pub, so one night he takes her along with him.

"Whit'll ye have?" he asks.

"Oh, I don't know. Same as you I suppose," she replies.

The husband orders a couple of straight whiskies and throws his down in one gulp. His wife watches him, takes a sip from her glass… and immediately spits it out.

"Yuck, it's horrible," she splutters. "I don't know how you can drink this stuff!"

"Well, there you go," cries the husband. "And you think I'm out enjoying myself every night!"

A NEW guy in town walks into a pub and notices a very large jar behind the bar… filled to the brim with ten pound notes. He reckons it must contain thousands of pounds, so he asks: "What's up with the jar?"

The barman replies: "You pay ten pounds and if you pass three tests then you get all of the money."

Man: "What are the three tests?"

Barman: "Pay first. Those are the rules."

So the guy gives him £10 and he adds it to the jar with the other notes

Barman: "Ok, here's what you have to do. First you have to drink a whole gallon of pepper tequila, the WHOLE thing at once AND you can't make a face while doing it.

"Second, there's a pit bull with a sore tooth chained up in the backyard. You have to remove the tooth with your bare hands. Third, there's a 90-year-old woman upstairs who's never had an orgasm in her life. You've got to make things right for her."

Man: "Well, I know I've paid my ten pounds but I'm not an idiot, I won't do it. You have to be nuts to drink a gallon of pepper tequila in the first place.

Barman: "Your call. But your money stays in the jar."

As time goes on and the man drinks a few, he shouts: "Wherrzza teeqeelah?"

He grabs the gallon of tequila with both hands, and downs it with a big slurp. Tears are streaming down his cheeks but he does not make a face…

Next he staggers out the back door and soon the people inside hear a huge scuffle going on. They hear barking, screams, yelps and growling – and eventually silence.

Just when they think the man must be dead, he staggers back into the bar, his shirt ripped and big scratches all over his body…

"Now," he says. "Where's the woman with the sore tooth?"

THIS guy goes into a bar and sees a man pounding shots of whisky as fast as the barman can pour them. He watches for a while then finally goes up to the drunk.

"What kind of a way is that to drink good whisky," he asks.

"It's the only way I can drink it since my accident," the man replies, throwing down two more shots in fast order.

"What kind of accident was that?"

The man guzzles another shot, shudders and then answers: "I once knocked over a drink with my elbow."

MAN in a pub orders six pints and six double whiskies!

The barman lines them up and says: "Man, you must've had one hell of a day!"

The guy answers: "Yeah, I just found out my older brother is gay."

Next day, the same guy comes into the same bar and orders the same drinks. The same barman is there and says: "Now what?"

The guy replies: "I just found out my younger brother is gay, too."

Next day, same guy, same bar, same drinks. The barman goes: "Damn! Doesn't anybody in your family like women?"

The man replies: "Yeah, my wife!"

MAN pulls a tiny piano and a one-foot high man from a bag and places them on the bar. The little guy jumps up and starts playing the piano.

The guy next to him is amazed and asks: "Where on earth did you get that?"

The first man says: "There's a genie living in a bottle next to the river. If you go there and rub the bottle, the genie will grant you one wish."

So the guy shoots off, finds the bottle near the river and rubs it. The genie appears and offers to grant one wish.

The guy says: "I want a million bucks."

The genie answers: "Go home and in one hour, look out of your window into your garden."

After an hour, the man looks outside and all he sees are DUCKS… everywhere.

He is angry and goes back to the bar to tell the first man: "I'm disgusted. I found the genie, but instead of one million BUCKS, he gave me one million DUCKS.

The other man says: "You're disgusted? Do you honestly think I asked that genie for a twelve-inch pianist?"

A MAN sits in a pub staring at his drink for half-an-hour.
A big trouble-maker goes up, lifts the glass and gulps it
down.

The poor man starts crying, and says: "This really is the
worst day of my life. First, I sleep in and am late for
work so my boss fires me. When I leave the building to
get my car, I find out it has been stolen.

"I get a taxi home and after it drops me off and zooms
away I realise that I've left my wallet and credit cards
on the seat. Then, when I go into my house, I find my
wife in bed with the gardener. I leave home and come
to this bar.

"And there I was, thinking about putting an end to my
life, when you show up and drink my poison…"

GUY goes up to a girl in a bar and
asks: "You want to play Magic?"
She says: "What's that?"
Guy answers: "We go to my house,
make passionate love and then
you disappear."

A MAN walks into a pub, and orders a beer. As he sits
there, the bowl of nuts on the bar tells him what a nice
shirt he is wearing. Disturbed by this, he goes to the
cigarette machine to buy a pack of smokes. As he
approaches the machine, it starts screaming and
shouting at him.

The barman apologises, saying: "The peanuts are
complimentary, but the cigarette machine is out of
order!"

A GUY walks into a bar with an octopus. He sits the octopus on a stool and announces that this is a very talented octopus, which can play any musical instrument in the world.

Everyone laughs at the man, calling him an idiot. So he says that he will wager £50 to anyone who has an instrument that the octopus can't play.

A guy walks up with a guitar and puts it beside the octopus. Immediately the octopus picks up the guitar and starts playing better than Eric Clapton. The guitar man pays up his £50.

Another guy comes up with a trumpet. This time the octopus plays like Miles Davis. This guy pays his £50.

Then a Scotsman hands over a set of bagpipes. The octopus fumbles with it for a minute and then sits down with a confused look.

"Ha," the Scot says. "Can ye no play it?"

The octopus looks at him and says: "Play it? I'm going to make love to it as soon as I figure out how to get these pyjamas off."

AN American walks into an Edinburgh pub and sits down next to a gorgeous woman. The first thing he notices are her trousers. They are skin-tight, high-waisted and have no obvious mechanism for opening them. After several minutes of wondering how she got them over her hips, he finally worked up the nerve to ask her.

"Excuse me miss, but how do you get into your pants," he asks.

"Well," she replies, "You can start by buying me a drink."

A MAN comes in to the room and says to his wife: "I'm going to the pub. Get your coat on."

The wife, overjoyed that he has included her in his activity replies: "Does that mean that you are taking me with you, darling?"

The husband replies: "No! I'm turning the heating off."

A COWBOY rides into town and stops at a saloon for a drink. When he finishes his drink, he finds his horse has been stolen.

He goes back into the bar, handily flips his gun into the air, catches it above his head without even looking and fires a shot into the ceiling.

"Which one of you sidewinders stole my hoss," he yells.

No-one answers.

"Alright, I'm gonna have another beer and if my hoss ain't back outside by the time I finish, I'm gonna do what I done in Texas! And I don't like to have to do what I done in Texas!"

Some of the locals shift restlessly.

He has another beer, walks outside, and his horse is back! He saddles-up and starts to ride out of town.

The bartender wanders out of the saloon and says:

"Stranger, before you go... what happened in Texas?"

The cowboy turned back and answers: "I had to walk home."

A MAN is sitting in the bar when he notices another patron a few stools away. The guy had a body like Arnie Schwarzenegger, but his head was the size of a thimble.

The first man says: "Excuse me for staring, but I can't help being curious as to why your body is so well developed, yet your head is so small?"

The man answers: "Buy me a drink and I'll tell you." So the drink is ordered and the story begins.

"I was in the navy and my ship was sunk by a torpedo. I was the only survivor and I managed to make it to a deserted island a few miles away.

"I had been there alone for several months and was sitting on the beach one day waiting for a bird or fish to come by so I would have something to eat. Looking up I saw a beautiful mermaid sunning herself on a nearby rock.

"She swam over to me and said that she was a magical mermaid and could grant me three wishes.

"I told her that I wanted be rescued. She slapped the water with her tail and a ship appeared, sailing straight for my island.

"Next I asked for a body like Arnie Schwarzenegger. Another slap of the tail and here it is. Then, noticing how beautiful she was and all my other wishes fulfilled I asked if I could make love to her. She said no... that it just wouldn't work with her being half fish and all.

"So I said, Well, how about a little head then?"

A baby seal waddles into a pub and the landlord asks: "What'll you have?"
The seal answers: "Whisky."
And the landlord says: "What sort?"
And the seal says: "Anything but Canadian Club!"

AFTER spending a happy evening drinking together, two acquaintances promise to meet again in ten years at the same bar, same time.

Ten years later, the first guy walks in, looks around, and sure enough, there is his friend on a bar stool. He clasps the old friend's hand and cries: "The day we left, I didn't think I'd really see you here!"

The friend looks up, stares, sways slightly and asks: "Who left?"

BILL was in the pub, bragging about his athletic prowess. None of the regulars challenged him, but a visitor piped up: "I'll bet 50 quid that I can push something in a wheelbarrow to the end of the road and that you can't wheel it back."

Bill looked at the skinny stranger and decided it wasn't much of a challenge. "I'll take you on," he said.

They borrowed a wheelbarrow and took it to the corner. "Now let's see what you're made of," taunted Bill.

"Okay," said the challenger. "Get in."

THIS guy's wife had just had a baby boy. The only thing wrong was that the kid was only a head. As time passed the head got older and older and his 18th birthday rolled around.

The man, being very proud of his son, took him out to have his first drink. So, he carried the head up to the pub and set him on the bar.

The barman came up and said: "What'll you have?"

The head replied: "Give me the best whisky in the house!"

His father helped him take a sip, and as soon as he did, WHAM… a pair of arms and shoulders popped out!

After seeing this, the kid was very happy and demanded another drink. After that a stomach popped out… after another, two legs popped out.

The boy was so excited that he ran out of the pub, into the street and was hit by a truck and killed instantly. The father and the barman come running out.

The father was kneeling over his son and crying and the barman said: "He should have quit while he was a head."

A BLONDE, a brunette, a redhead, a vicar, a priest, a rabbi, two giraffes and a duck, a farmer, a lawyer, an accountant, a Mexican, an Indian, a Chinaman, an Irishman, an Englishman an American and a Scotsman walked into a pub.

The barman said: "Hang on a minute, is this some sort of joke?"

THE BEER PRAYER:

Our lager, Which art in barrels,
Hallowed be thy drink.
Thy will be drunk, (I will be drunk),
At home as it is in the tavern.
Give us this day our foamy head,
And forgive us our spillage,
As we forgive those who spill against us.
And lead us not to incarceration,
But deliver us from hangovers.
For thine is the beer, the bitter,
and the lager.
Barmen.

A POLICEMAN pulls over this car which has been weaving in and out of the lanes. He goes up to the window and says: "Sir, I need you to blow into this breathalyser tube."

The man says: "Sorry officer I can't do that. I am an asthmatic. If I do that I'll have a bad asthma attack."

"Okay, fine. I need you to come down to the station to give a blood sample."

I can't do that either. I am a haemophiliac. If I do that, I'll bleed to death."

"Well, then we need a urine sample."

"Sorry officer I can't do that either. I am also a diabetic. If I do that I'll get really low blood sugar."

"Alright then, I need you to come out here and walk this white line."

"I can't do that, officer."

"Why not?"

"Because I'm drunk."

A MAN walks into a bar and the barman asks: "What'll you have?"

The guy answers: "A whisky, please."

The barman hands him the drink and says: "That'll be £2."

The man replies: "What are you talking about? I don't owe you anything for this."

A lawyer, sitting nearby and overhearing the conversation, says to the barman: "You know, he's got you there. In the original offer, which constitutes a binding contract upon acceptance, there was no stipulation of remuneration."

The barman's not impressed, but says to the man: "Okay, you beat me for a drink, but don't ever let me catch you in here again."

The next day, the same guy walks into the bar. The barman says: "What the hell are you doing in here? I can't believe you've got the nerve to come back!"

The guy says: "What are you talking about? I've never been in this place in my life!"

To which the barman replies: "I'm very sorry, but this is uncanny. You must have a double."

The man replies: "Thank you! Make it a whisky."

A SANDWICH walked into a bar. But the barman said, "Sorry, we don't serve food here!"

SCOTT is in a boozer after work for a couple of shandies when he notices a guy slumped over the bar totally wasted. Scott walks over and decides to help the poor bugger out.

So he looks in the guy's wallet to find out where he lives. Then he drags the drunk off the barstool and tries to get him to stand up. But every time this happens the drunk falls to the floor.

Scott eventually gets the drunk to the car. When they arrive at the drunks house, Scott pulls the guy out of the car and tries to help him to his front door but the guy keeps collapsing.

Scott knocks on the front door and a woman answers. Scott explains that he has brought her husband home.

"Thanks very much" says the woman, "But where the hell is his wheelchair?"

MAN runs into a pub and says to the barman: "Give me twenty double vodkas, quick!"

The barman pours out the drinks, and the guy swallows them as fast as he can.

The barman says: "Wow. I never saw anybody drink that fast."

The guy replies: "Well, you'd drink that fast too if you had what I have."

The barman says: "Oh my God! What is it? What do you have?"

The guy says: "Fifty pence."

A GUY is sitting at the bar talking to his hand. The barman asks what he's doing and the guy says: "I'm using the telephone."

The barman looks at him as if he's crazy and says: "No, you aren't, you are just talking into your hand."

The guy says: "No, I really am having a phone conversation. I had a micro chip and transmitter installed in my hand last week."

The barman shrugs and goes about his business. A few minutes later the guy disappears into the toilet and he's gone about an hour. The barman starts to get worried so he goes into the toilet to see if the guy is okay.

When he gets there, he finds the guy standing in the middle of the bathroom with both hands in the air, his trousers down around his ankles and a roll of toilet paper stuck in his backside.

The bartman is flabbergasted and so he asks: "What are you doing now?"

The guy replies: "I'm waiting for a fax."

A SET of jump-leads walk into a Glasgow pub.
The barman says: "I'll serve you, but don't start anything."

GUY goes up to the bar and orders two double vodkas.
   He drinks the first and pours the second on his right
   hand. He then orders a second round, drinks the first
   and again pours the second on his right hand.
The barman sees this and becomes curious as the guy
   orders a third round and does the exact same thing.
So the barman asks the guy: "Hey pal, I hope you don't
   mind me asking but why the waste of good vodka?"
The man says: "I'm trying to get my date drunk!"

**SITTING in the pub, glum George told the barman
   that he was drinking to forget the heartbreak of his
   broken engagement.**
**"Well," said George, "would you marry someone who
   didn't know the meaning of the word faithful. And
   who went crazy when the subject of fidelity came up?"**
"No way in hell," the barman said.
"Well," said George, "neither would my fiancée."

MAN walks into a bar and orders martini after martini,
   each time removing the olives and placing them in a
   jar.
When the jar was filled with olives and all the drinks
   consumed, the guy started to leave with the jar.
"Excuse me," said a customer, who was puzzled about
   what the guy had done. "What was that all about?"
"Nothing," said the guy. "My wife just sent me out for a
   jar of olives."

A DRUNK is sitting at one end of the bar, while at the
other end is a really ugly woman. The barman asks if
anyone wants another drink? They both raise their
arms and the drunk and the barman notice the woman
had huge tufts of matted hair under her armpit.

The drunk insists on paying for the drink for the ballerina
at the end of the bar. The barman is confused with this
statement but reckons it is just the drink speaking.

A short time later the barman had announces: "Last
orders." Again, both the drunk and the ugly woman
raise their arms and the drunk again offers to buy the
ballerina's drink.

This time the barman serves the woman but tells the
drunk that he's had enough.

He says: "I know you're drunk and are having difficulty
seeing straight but why do you keep calling that
woman a ballerina?"

The drunk slurs: "Any woman who can lift her leg that
high must be a ballerina."

A GUY is driving through the prairies of the USA and
stops at a small town. He goes into a bar, orders a
drink, and lights up a cigar. As he sips his drink, he
stands there quietly blowing smoke rings.

After he blew nine or ten smoke rings into the air, an
angry American Indian stomps up to him and says:
"One more remark like that and I'll smash your face
in!"

A DRUNK is walking down the street. He sees this nun, runs up and knocks her over. He says: "You don't feel so tough now, do you, Batman?"

A MAN is sitting at a bar one night, wearing a fancy new watch, covered with buttons and lights and dials. The woman next to him says: "Wow, that's a really fancy watch."

"Thanks," says the guy. "It's the cutting edge of technology. I can telepathically ask this watch anything I want to know, and it'll answer me, telepathically."

"Rubbish, you're having me on," says the girl.

"No, it's true," says that guy. "Look, tell you what, I'll prove it. I'll ask it if you've got any panties on."

The guy scrunches up his eyes for a moment, as if concentrating hard to talk to his watch, then opens them and says: "No, my watch claims you haven't got any panties on."

"Well, it's wrong," says the girl. "I am wearing panties."

"Damn," says the guy, slapping his watch, "It's an hour fast!"

A DRUNKEN lout sits next to a young woman at the bar and says: "Sweetheart, I'd really like to get into those pants of yours."

"Thanks," she replies, "but I've already got an asshole in there."

BEER WARNING

MEN, be more alert and cautious when being offered a drink by a girl. There is a drug called "beer" that is essentially in liquid form.

The most effective varieties are being shipped in from other countries. "Beer" is now being used by female sexual predators at parties to convince their male victims to have sex with them.

The shocking statistic is that this "beer" is available virtually anywhere! All girls have to do is buy a "beer" or two for almost any bloke and simply ask him home for no-strings-attached sex.

Men are literally rendered helpless against such attacks. Please, forward this warning to every man you know. There is safety in numbers...

AN IRISHMAN, an Englishman and a Scotsman go into a pub and each orders a pint of Guinness. Just as the barman hands them over, three flies buzz down and land in each of the pints.

The Englishman looks disgusted, pushes his pint away and demands another pint. The Scotsman picks out the fly, shrugs, and takes a long swallow.

The Irishman reaches into the glass, pinches the fly between his fingers and shakes him while yelling: "Spit it out, ya bastard! Spit it out!"

A MAN walks into a bar with his horse and offers £100 to anybody who can make the horse laugh. One guy whispers something in the horse's ear and the horse starts to laugh.

The following week, the man is back in the bar with his horse again and offers £200 to anyone who can make the horse cry. The guy who won the previous bet takes the horse off to the bathroom. When they come back, the horse is crying his eyes out.

Amazed, the owner asks the man how he did it.

The man says: "Last week, I told the horse that I had a bigger pecker than he did. This week, I showed it to him."

HOW many men does it take to open a beer?
None. It should be opened by the time she brings it to you!

A SEXY lady walks up to the bar and motions the barman over. She starts to run her fingers through his hair and asks to speak to the manager. The barman says: "He isn't here but I can do anything the manager can do for you."

By this time the lady is running her hands down his face and into his mouth and is letting him suck her fingers.

She says: "You're sure he isn't here?"

The bartender says: "Yes, I'm very sure."

The lady says: "Well, I just wanted to tell him there's no toilet paper or soap in the ladies' toilet."

THERE'S a wee man sitting in a bar drinking a beer. A while later a huge hardcase walks up to the little guy and karate chops him in the neck. The little guy falls off his stool and when he gets up the big guy says: "That was a karate chop from Korea."

The big guy goes to the toilet and the wee man orders himself another beer. About 20 minutes later the trouble-maker comes back and karate chops him in the neck again. The wee man gets up and dusts himself off and the big guy tells him: "That was a karate chop from China."

The wee man gets up and decides he isn't going to take any more of this, so he leaves the pub. About an hour later the wee man comes back and he hits the big guy over the head, knocking him out cold.

Then the wee man says to the barman: "Tell him that was a crowbar from B&Q."

A DRUNK is driving through the city and his car is weaving violently all over the road. A policeman pulls him over and asks: "Where have you been?"

"I've been to the pub," slurs the drunk.

"Well," says the cop, "it looks like you've had quite a few."

"I did alright," the drunk says with a smile.

"Did you know," says the cop, standing straight and folding his arms, "that a few miles back, your wife fell out of your car?"

"Oh, thank heavens," sighs the drunk. "For a minute there, I thought I'd gone deaf."

Men & Women

Sex? Don't knock it till you've tried it. It's been making us laugh since Helen of Troy... the face that launched a thousand zips!

ONE night, Jimmy passed by his wee boy's room and heard his son praying: "God bless Mummy, Daddy, and Grandma. Ta ta, Grandpa."

Puzzled, Jimmy didn't quite know what this meant but was glad his son was praying. The next morning, they found Grandpa dead on the floor of a heart attack. The father reassured himself that it was just a coincidence, but was still a bit spooked.

The next night, he heard his son praying again: "God bless Mummy and Daddy. Ta ta, Grandma."

The father was worried, but decided to wait until morning. Sure enough, when he woke up Grandma was on the floor, dead of a heart attack.

Really scared now, Jim decided to wait outside his son's door the next night. And sure enough, the boy started to pray: "God bless Mummy. Ta ta, Daddy."

Now the father was crapping his pants. He stayed up all night, and went to the doctor's early the next day to make sure his health was fine. When he came home, his wife was waiting on the porch. She said: "Thank God you're here – we could really use your help! We found the milkman dead on our porch this morning!"

TED and Julie go to bed with one another for the first time.
Julie: I think I should warn you, I've got acute angina
Ted: You're tits aren't bad either.

A BOY walks into a chemist's and asks for a box of condoms.
The pharmasist grins and winks and says, "Okay, what size?"
The boy looks him in the eyes and says, "Assorted. They're for my sister."

A NEWLY-married man was discussing his honeymoon. He says to his mate: "Last night, I rolled over, tapped my beautiful young wife on the shoulder, gave her a wink, and we had ourselves a performance!

"Later, about 2am, I rolled over, gave my sweetie a nudge, and we had ourselves another performance. Well, being so newly married and not yet tired of the task, I waited quietly in bed while she slept until I couldn't wait any longer. It was 4am when I gave her a little nudge. She opened her blue eyes and smiled sweetly. We immediately had ourselves a rehearsal."

"A rehearsal?" his pal asks, "Don't you mean a performance?"

"No, because a rehearsal is when nobody comes".

A HUSBAND comes home early from work and finds his next door neighbour in bed with his missus.

"I can't believe you, you tosser," he screams at his neighbour. "I've lent you cash, I've loaned you my motor, after all I've done for you ... and stop doing that while I'm talking to you!"

A FATHER and son go into the supermarket when they happen upon the condom shelf. The son asks his father why there are so many different boxes . The father replies: "Well, you see that three-pack? That's for when you're at high school. You have two for Friday night and one for Saturday night."

The son then asks his father: "What's the six-pack for?"

The father replies: "Well, that's for when you're at university. You have two for Friday night, two for Saturday night and two for Sunday morning."

Then the son asks his father what the 12-pack is for.

The father replies: "Well, that's for when you're married. You have one for January, one for February, one for March, one for ..."

A MAN and a woman entered a lift on the top floor of the Canary Wharf tower. As soon as the door closed, a cable snapped and the elevator started plummeting toward the ground.

The woman, realising she had only seconds to live, ripped off her dress, threw it in the corner, and said, "MAKE ME FEEL LIKE A WOMAN!"

So the man ripped off his clothes, chucked them in the corner and shouted: "FOLD THEM, YOU LAZY BITCH."

JOE stopped at his favourite pub after a hard day's work to relax. He noticed a man next to him order a shot and a beer. The man drank the shot, chased it with the beer and then looked into his shirt pocket.

This continued several times before Joe's curiosity got the best of him. He leaned over to the bloke and said: "I couldn't help but notice your little ritual. Why do you look into your pocket after having a drink?"

The man replied: "There's a photo of my wife in there, and when she starts lookin' good, I go home!"

ANGUS has three girlfriends but doesn't know which one to marry. So he decides to give them £5,000 each and see how they spend it.

The first one goes out and gets a total makeover. She gets new clothes, a new hairdo, manicure, pedicure – the works – and tells Angus: "I spent the money so I could look pretty for you, because I love you so much."

The second girl went out and bought new golf clubs, a CD player, a television and a stereo and gives them to the man. She says: "I bought these gifts for you with the money because I love you so much."

The third one takes the £5,000 and invests it in the stock market, doubles her investment, returns the £5,000 to the man and reinvests the rest. She says: "I am investing the rest of the money for our future because I love you so much."

Angus thought long and hard about how each of the women spent the money. He finally decided to marry the one with the biggest tits.

A YOUNG man is lost in a forest when he comes upon
a small house. Knocking on the door he is greeted by a
very old Chinese man with a long grey beard.

"I'm lost," said the man. "Can I stay here tonight?" The
old man replied: "Yes, but on one condition – if you lay
a finger on my daughter I will inflict upon you the
three worst Chinese tortures known to man."

The man agreed and entered the house. Over dinner, the
daughter appeared. She was young, beautiful, had a
fantastic body – and flirted with her guest throughout
the meal, making it clear she wanted him.

Remembering the old man's warning he ignored her and
went to bed alone. But during the night he could bear
it no longer and crept into her room for a night of
passion. He was careful to keep everything quiet so the
old man wouldn't hear and, near dawn, he crept back
to his room, exhausted but happy.

He woke to feel a pressure on his chest. Opening his eyes
he saw a large rock on his chest with a note on it that
read: "Chinese Torture 1: Large rock on chest."

"Well, that's pretty crap," he thought. "If that's the worst
the old man can do, I don't have much to worry about."

He picked the boulder up, walked over to the window
and threw out the rock. As he did so, he noticed
another note on it that read: "Chinese Torture 2: Rock
tied to left testicle."

In a panic, he glanced down and saw that the rope was
already getting close to taut. Figuring a few broken
bones were better than castration he jumped out of the
window. As he fell, he saw a large sign that read,
"Chinese Torture 3: Right testicle tied to bed post."

A WOMAN in a coma is getting a sponge bath from the hospital's nurses. One of them is washing between her legs and notices there is a response on the monitor when she is being touched.

They go to her husband and explain what happened, telling him: "It might sound crazy but maybe a little oral sex will bring her out of the coma."

The husband is sceptical but they assure him they will close the curtains for privacy. Besides it's worth a try. The hubby finally agrees and goes into his wife's room.

After a few minutes the woman's monitor flat lines, no pulse and no heart rate.

The nurses run into the room. The husband is pulling up his trousers and says "I think she choked."

OLD Albert and Senga had been married for 50 years. On the morning of their Golden Wedding they were sitting at the breakfast table when Bert says to his wife: "Just think, we've been married for 50 years."

"Yeah," she replied. "Fifty years ago we were sitting here at this breakfast table together."

"I know," the old man said. "We were probably sitting here naked as the day we were born."

"Well," Senga says, "What do you say ... should we get naked?" Where upon the two stripped to the buff and sat down at the table.

"You know," the old dear whispers. "My nipples are as hot for you today as they were fifty years ago."

"I wouldn't be surprised," replies Bert. "One's in your coffee and the other is in your porridge."

A YOUNG couple were in a car, driving down the motorway, when the guy says to the girl: "If I go 100 miles an hour, will you take off your clothes?"

She agrees and when the speedo hits 100 she starts to strip. But he is so busy staring at her he flips the car.

The girl is thrown clear without a scratch but her clothes and her boyfriend are trapped in the wreckage. "Go get help," he pleads. She replies, "I can't, I'm naked."

He points to his shoe that was thrown clear and says "Cover your snatch with that and go get help."

She takes the shoe, covers herself and runs to the nearest petrol station. When she arrives she is frantic and yells to the mechanic, "HELP! My boyfriend's stuck!"

He looks down at the shoe covering her crotch and shakes his head: "Sorry miss. He's too far in."

Did you hear about the fantastic new bra for middle-aged women?
It's called the Sheepdog ...
because it rounds them up and points them in the right direction.

A BAKERY owner hires a young girl with a penchant for very short skirts. One day a young man enters the shop, glances at the assistant and studies the loaves behind the counter.

"I'd like some raisin bread, please," the man asks.

The new girl nods and shuffles up a ladder to reach the raisin bread located on the very top shelf.

The man, standing below her, gets a top-quality gander as she retrieves the bread.

A small group of male customers gather around the young man, looking in the same direction. Pretty soon everyone is asking for raisin bread, just to see the clerk climb up and down.

After a few trips the assistant is irritated. She stops at the top of the ladder and glares at the men below. She notices a old man standing in the crowd.

"Is yours raisin too?" she yells.

"No," croaks the feeble old man. "But it's startin' to twitch."

"I'm going to divorce my missus," said Paul to his mates in the pub one night.
"Her dirty habits disgust me. Why only yesterday I went to pee in the sink and it was still full of dirty dishes."

AN ELDERLY couple are watching one of those
television preachers on TV one night. The preacher
faces the camera, and announces:
"My friends, I would like to share my healing powers
with everyone watching this programme. Place one
hand on top of your TV, and the other on the part of
your body which ails you and I will heal you."
The old woman has been having terrible stomach
problems, so she places one hand on the television,
and her other hand on her stomach.
Meanwhile, her husband approaches the television,
placing one hand on top of the TV and his other
hand on his groin.
With a frown his wife says: "Ernest, he is talking
about healing the sick, not raising the dead."

SHORTLY after a new police
chief constable took office, the
local knocking shop was raided
and the girls were lined up
outside for questioning and
transport to the police station.
A little old lady chanced to walk
by while this was happening,
and noticing the "line-up" asked what was happening.
As a joke, one of the 'chicks' told her they were
standing in line for free lollipops.
A few minutes later, a constable approached the elderly
woman and asked: "Aren't you a little bit old for this?"
"Officer," she softly replied with a sweet smile. "As long
as they keep making them, I'll keep sucking them."

A MAN was walking along the street when he saw a ladder up into the sky. Curious, he climbed the ladder and reached a cloud, upon which sat a fat, ugly woman. "Do me or climb the ladder to success," she said.

"No contest", thought the man, so he climbed up to the next cloud where he met a slightly thinner woman, who was also easier on the eye.

"Do me hard or climb the ladder to success," she said.

"Well," thought the man, "might as well carry on."

On the next cloud was an even more shapely, attractive burd who trotted out the standard line.

"Do me now or climb the ladder to success," she said.

Again he turned her down, reckoning his chances were getting better the further he went. On the next cloud was a real cracker. Slim, attractive, the lot and she moaned: "Do me now or climb the ladder to success."

Being a gambling man, he decided to climb again. But when he reached the next cloud, there was a hairy 18-stone ugly bloke with flies buzzing around his head.

"Who are you?" the shocked cloud climber asked.

"Hello" said the ugly fat man. "I'm Cess!"

41

A RANDY teenager goes to a chemist to buy condoms.
The pharmacist says they are in packs of three, nine or
12 and asks which the young man wants.

"Well," he said, "I've been seeing this girl for a while and
she's gagging for it. I want the condoms because I
think tonight's the night. We're having dinner with her
parents and then we're going out after that.

"And I reckon I'm going to get lucky, so you better give
me the 12 pack because we'll be at it all night."

That evening before dinner he surprises everyone by
offering to say Grace. He begins the prayer which lasts
for several minutes.

The girl leans over and says: "You never told me you
were so religious."

He leans over to her and whispers: "You never told me
your father was a chemist."

A JUMBO jet was about to land but the pilot had
forgotten to switch off the intercom.

"First thing I'm going to do is have an ice cold pint of
beer then I'm going to ride the ass off that
little stewardess," he tells the co-pilot.
The horrified flight attendant
made a mad dash to the
cockpit to warn the pilot.
A little old lady sitting by
the aisle said: "There's
no need to rush my
dear. He said he was
going to have a beer
first."

A WOMAN
was horrified to
find out that she
was pregnant.
"When did you have
your last check-up?"
asked her doctor.
"Check up" screamed the
woman. "I've had a
Scotsman, an Englishman, a
Frenchman and a Spaniard,
but never had a Czech!"

THREE friends play golf together every Saturday. One day a guy, by himself, asks if he can join them. The pals agree and strike up a conversation with the stranger and ask what he does for a living.

The guy says: "I'm a hitman. My gun is in my golf bag. If you don't believe me take a look."

One of the friends checks it out. He opens the bag and, sure enough, there is a rifle with a huge telescopic sight.

He's well impressed and asks to look through the sight at his house and the hitman agrees.

The guy looks for a second and says: "Yes, I can see right into my bedroom. There's my wife, naked. Hold on. There's my next-door neighbour. And he's naked too."

The man is upset and asks the hitman how much it would be for a hit. The hitman replies: "I get £1000 every time I pull the trigger."

The guy responds: "£1000? Well, OK. I want two hits. I want you to shoot my wife in the mouth. She's always nagging and I can't stand it. Then, I want you to shoot my neighbour's dick off for screwing with my wife."

The hitman agrees and takes aim. But after five minutes he still hasn't fired. The husband starts to get really impatient and asks: "What are you waiting for?"

The hitman replies: "Be quiet ... I'm about to save you a thousand quid."

**WHAT does a man
with a 10-inch prick
have for breakfast?
Well, this morning I
had toast, cereal,
coffee ...**

A HUGE-breasted girl wearing a skimpy bikini on the
beach attracted the interests of a dirty old man who
offered her £20 quid to fondle her boobs.

Not surprisingly, the beach babe was horrified and
yelled: "Get away from me, you old perv."

The old man was not so easily put off and upped his
offer, saying: "I want to feel your breasts – I will give
you £100!"

"No! Get away from me!" she repeated.

"£200," he offered.

This time she paused and thought about his bid before
again telling him to get lost.

"£500 if you give me a grope," he begged.

She thought to herself: "Well he is old and he seems
harmless enough... and £500 IS a lot of money...
"Okay. But only for a minute," she told him.

She loosened her bikini top and he slid his gnarled old
hands underneath. Then he started groaning: "Oh my
God. Oh my God. Oh my God."

Out of curiosity, she asked him, "Why do you keep
saying, 'Oh my God, oh my God'?"

While continuing to feel her breasts he answered: "Oh
my God. Oh my God. Oh my God. Oh my God. Oh
my God. Where am I ever going to get £500?"

DAVIE was sitting reading his Daily Record one morning, minding his own business, when his wife sneaks up behind him and whacks him on the back of his head with a frying pan.

Tam says: "What was that for?"

His wife replies: "What were you doing with a piece of paper in your trouser pocket with the name Tracey written on it?"

Quick as a flash, he explains: "Remember two weeks ago when I went to Ayr races? Tracey was the name of one of the horses I bet on."

The wife looks all satisfied, apologises for crowning him, and goes off to do work around the house.

Three days later Davie is once again sitting in his chair reading and she repeats the frying pan swatting.

He angrily yells: "What the hell was that for this time?"

His wife replies: "Your horse called."

ONE day a little boy named Bobby surprised his mum
and dad having sex and asked what they were doing.
"We're playing poker and your mummy's the wild card,"
replied his dad.
So Bobby walked out and went into his brother's room
and saw his brother and his girlfriend having sex.
"What are you doing?" asked Bobby. "We're playing
poker and she's the wild card," replied his brother.
So Bobby walked out and went to his room. Later on
Bobby's father walked in on his lad having a wank.
"What are you doing?" yelled his father.
Bobby replied: "I'm playing poker!"
"But where is your wild card?"
Bobby replied: "With a hand like this one who needs a
wild card."

HEARD the one about the tart
who went on a fishing trip
with six men?
She came home with a red
snapper.

TWO women were having lunch and discussing the
merits of cosmetic surgery.
The first woman says: "I'm getting a boob job."
The second woman says: "That's nothing, I'm thinking
of having my asshole bleached!"
To which the first replies: "Strange, I just can't picture
your husband as a blond!"

A MARRIED couple are in their car driving down the
M8 at 55 mph. The husband is behind the wheel. His
wife looks over at him and says: "Look Bill, I know
we've been married for 15 years, but I want a divorce."
The husband says nothing but slowly increases speed to
60 mph.
Then she confesses: "I don't want you to try to talk me
out of it. The truth is I've been having an affair with
your best friend and he's a better lover than you."
Again the husband stays quiet and just speeds up as his
anger increases.
She says: "As part of the divorce I want to keep the
house."
Again Bill speeds up and now is
doing 70 mph.
She goes on: "I want the kids
too."
The husband just keeps driving
faster, and faster – now he's
up to 80 mph.
She says: "Also I want to keep the
car, our savings and all the credit cards too. And, sorry,
I want to have custody of the cat and dog."
Finally she says: "Is there anything you want?"
Poor Billy has turned bright red and slowly the car starts
to drift towards a flyover which is supported by giant
concrete pillars.
The husband says: "No, I've got everything I need."
She asks: "What's that?"
And just before they hit the wall at 90 mph, Bill says:
"I've got the driver's airbag!"

Charlie
loved to watch
his wedding video
backwards so he
could see himself
walking out of the
church a free
man.

A YOUNG bride-to-be was preparing for her wedding night and asked her mum to buy a long black negligee and place it in her suitcase so it would not wrinkle.

Well, her old dear forgot until the last minute and the only thing she could find was a short pink nightie. Nevertheless, she bought it and chucked it in the case.

After the wedding the bride and groom enter their hotel room. The groom was a bit shy so he told his new wife not to peek while he got ready for bed.

While he was in the bathroom, the bride opened her suitcase and saw the negligee her maw had thrown in. She shouted: "Oh no! It's short, pink, and wrinkled!"

Her groom cried out: "I told you not to peek!"

WHAT are the three words you don't want to hear while you are having sex? "Honey, I'm home!"

DAVE asks his wife, Anne, what she wants for their 40th wedding anniversary.

"Would you like a mink coat, a diamond ring or perhaps a new Mercedes sports car?" he offers.

"No," she responds.

"What about a holiday home in the country?" he asks.

Again she rejects him before taking a deep breath and saying: "Actually, I'd like a divorce."

"Sorry, I wasn't planning to spend that much," says Dave.

THREE women were sitting around throwing back a few drinks and talking about their sex lives.

One woman said: "I call my husband the dentist. Nobody can drill like he does."

The second woman giggled and confessed: "I call my husband the miner because of his incredible shaft."

The third woman quietly sipped her whiskey until her friend asked: "So what do you call your husband?"

She frowned and said: "The postman."

"Why the postman?"

"Because he always delivers late and half the time it's in the wrong box."

WHY does a man's penis have a hole in it?
So he can get oxygen to his brain.

A YOUNG couple were very nervous on their first night together.

He parked the car in Lovers' Lane, put his arm around her and whispered in her ear: "Would you like to get in the backseat?"

"No," she replied. "I'd rather stay in the front seat with you."

HOW many men do you need to screw on a light bulp?
One. They'll screw anything.

A DOCTOR, a bank manager and a brickie were in a pub having a bevvy.

After a sip of his martini, the doctor said: "You know, tomorrow is my anniversary. I got my wife a diamond ring and a new BMW. I figure that if she doesn't like the diamond ring, she will at least like her new car, and she will know that I love her."

After finishing his Scotch, the bank manager said: "Well, on my last anniversary, I got my wife a string of pearls and a trip to the Bahamas. I figured if she didn't like the pearls, she would at least like the trip, and she would know that I love her."

The brickie then took a swig from his beer, and said: "Yeah, well for my anniversary, I got my old lady a tee-shirt and a vibrator. I figured if she didn't like the tee-shirt, she could go screw herself."

A GUY gets a prescription for Viagra and takes a tablet shortly before his wife is expected home from work.

Well, the minutes go by, the man is all worked up and raring to go – but there's no sign of his wife.

Then she calls him on her mobile and explains: "Traffic is terrible, darling. I won't be there for about an hour and a half."

The man, frustrated, calls his doctor for advice. "What should I do?" he asks. The doc replies: "It would be a shame to waste it. Do you have a housekeeper?"

"Yes" the man replied.

"Well, maybe you can occupy yourself with her instead?" said the Doctor. The man then replied with dismay: "But I don't need Viagra with the housekeeper ..."

TWO men are fishing in a boat under a bridge. One looks up and sees a funeral procession starting across the bridge. He stands up, takes off his cap, and bows his head. The procession crosses the bridge and the man puts on his cap, picks up his rod and reel, and continues fishing.

The other guy says: "That was touching. I didn't know you had it in you."

The first man responds: "Well, I guess it was the thing to do. After all, I was married to her for 40 years."

THIS old man goes to the doctor's.
"Help, Doc. I just got married to this beautiful 21-year-old woman. She is hot and all she wants to do is have sex all day long."
"So what's the problem?"
"I can't remember where I live."

ONE day Jock, known for always being broke and shabby, walks into his local pub. One of the other regulars, notices his new clothes and brand new motorbike and asks where he got them. Jock, with a big, proud smile on his face explains: "I was walking down the road, when all of a sudden a girl rides up on this shiny new motorbike.

She gets off her bike, throws off all her clothes and says: "Take what you want."

So I did.

A HOUSEWIFE is tired of being alone everyday with her husband at work and her three daughters in school. So she decides to get a pet to keep her company.

She goes to the petshop and says she wants a talking parrot. The man behind the counter tells her that they have one talking parrot but warns that she wouldn't like him.

"Why not," she asks.

"Well, he has been around a bit and has picked up some colorful language and you did say that you have a family," he replied.

"Well, my girls are old enough and they've heard it all. Just let me see the parrot."

The man shows her the parrot and she insists on buying it right away. When she gets home she covers the cage with a towel and goes off to make dinner for the family.

When she uncovers the cage next day the parrot looks around and squawks: "Brawkk! New place. New Madam. Morning Madam."

"Uh, morning parrot," she says.

A few minutes later her daughters come down stairs, dressed and ready for school.

"Brawkk! New place. New Madam. New Girls. Morning Girls."

"Morning Parrot," they reply.

Soon the man of the house comes down, unshaven and in his bathrobe.

"Brawkk! New place. New Madam. New Girls. Same old customers. Morning Phil!"

Good Sports

Sport and sports people are often the butt of some biting humour. And why not? How else would I make a living?

A GUY walks into a bar with his pet dog. The barman says: "Sorry. No pets allowed."

The man replied, "This is a special dog. Turn on the Aberdeen game and you'll see."

The barman, anxious to see what will happen, turns on the TV. The guy said: "Watch. Whenever the Dons have an attempt on goal, my dog does flips."

Aberdeen keep firing shot upon shot at the goal and the dog keeps flipping and jumping.

"Wow! That's one hell of a dog you got there. What happens when Aberdeen score?"

The man replies: "I don't know. I've only had him for seven years!"

HOW many Man Utd fans does it take to change a lightbulb? One to change the lightbulb, and one to drive down to London to pick him up.

WHILE out one morning in the park, a jogger found a brand new tennis ball. Since no-one was around, he slipped it into the pocket of his shorts.

On his way home, he stopped at the pedestrian crossing, waiting for the lights to change. A blonde girl standing next to him eyed the large bulge in his shorts.

"What's that?" she asked, her eyes gleaming with lust.

"Tennis ball," came the breathless reply.

"Oh," said the blonde girl sympathetically, "that must be painful. I had tennis elbow once."

SATAN and St Peter were arguing one day about football. Satan proposed a game that would be played on neutral grounds between a select team from the Heavenly Host and the devil's own hand-picked boys.

"Very well," said the gatekeeper of Heaven. "But I hope that you realise we've got all the good players and the best coaches."

"I know, but it's okay." Satan answered. "We've got all the referees."

How can you tell the Elephant Man is a Kilmarnock supporter? Because he looks like one

A SUPPORTER arrived at the ground one Saturday to find the place empty. He went to the office and asked: "What time does the match start?"

"There's no match today," replied the official.

"But there's always a match on Saturday afternoon," said the fan.

"Watch my lips," shouted the irate official. "There is no M-A-T-F-C-H today!"

"Well for your information," the fan shouted back, "there's no F in match."

"That's exactly what I've been trying to tell you!" yelled the official.

THERE was once a fanatical Rangers supporter who thought of nothing but football. He read about it, watched all the games on the box and went to Ibrox as often as he possibly could.

Eventually his poor wife could stand it no longer. One night she said: "I honestly believe you love Rangers more than you love me!"

"No woman," said the fan. "I love Celtic more than I love you!"

> **A YOUNG boy managed to get lost at a football match. He saw a cop and said: "Excuse me mister, I've lost my dad."**
> **The policeman asked: "What's he like?"**
> **The kid thinks a bit and says: "Beer and loose women."**

A WOMAN was reading her newspaper and pointed out an article to her hubby.

"Look at this dear," she said. "There's a story about a man who traded his wife for a Motherwell season ticket. You wouldn't do a thing like that, would you?"

"Of course I wouldn't," replied the husband.

"The season's almost over."

> **AN ANXIOUS woman goes to her doctor after a night of dodgy sex.**
> **"Doctor," she asks nervously, "can you get pregnant from anal intercourse?"**
> **"Certainly," replies the doctor. "Where do you think Hibs fans come from?"**

GEORGE looks like a golf pro in his designer outfit but
   he slices his first drive deep into the woods.
Rather than accept a penalty, he decides to try using an
   iron to get back on the fairway. His ball ricochets off a
   tree and strikes him on the forehead, killing him.
When he arrives at the Pearly Gates, St Peter greets him.
   "You look like a golfer. Are you any good?"
George replies: "Yes. I got here in TWO, didn't I?"

**DID you hear that
   the Post Office
   just recalled their
   latest stamps?
They had pictures
   of Rangers
   players on them.
And people couldn't
   figure out which
   side to spit on.**

**Did you hear about
   the footballer who
   went on a date
   with a referee's
   daughter?
She booked him
   for handling,
   interference, and
   trying to pull off
   her jersey.**

A HUSBAND and wife are enjoying a round of golf
   when the woman was stung by an angry wasp as she
   about to hit a drive.
The sting started to swell up really badly so her worried
   husband ran back to the clubhouse to get a doctor.
"Doc, the missus has just been stung by a wasp and it's
   starting to swell," said the husband.
"OK," said the doc. "Where was she stung?"
"Between the first and second holes"
"Wow," said the doctor. "She must have a wide stance."

A SCOUT for Celtic is talent-spotting in war-torn Kosovo and sees a kid with amazing talent.

The lad jumps at the chance of escaping his troubled country and starting a new life in Scotland.

In the league that year, the Old Firm are neck-and-neck at the top entering the last day of the season. To make matters more tense, Celtic and Rangers are playing each other – winner takes all.

At 2-2 going into the last minute of the game, the ball drops to Dragan, Celtic's new Kosovan prodigy, who drifts past five Rangers players and unleashes a belter into the top corner to score the winning goal.

Soon after, there are wild celebrations as Celtic celebrate their win.

Dragan is hailed as a hero and invited by the manager to guzzle champagne back in the dressing room with the rest of the team.

However, before doing this, Dragan phones his mother to tell her the good news.

He says: "Guess what mum. You won't believe what happened today. We won the game and I scored the winning goal. I'm a hero!"

His maw interrupts: "You selfish bugger. You are always thinking of yourself.

"Do you have any idea what happened to us today? Your father has been killed, your sister was raped and taken from us, and our house has been burnt to the ground!"

"But mum, you are not being fair. You're acting as if all this was my fault," says Dragan.

"Your damn right it is. You're the tosser who got us to move to Glasgow in the first place."

AROUND THE GROUNDS:

WHAT'S the difference between Dunfermline's squad
and a puddle?
A puddle has more depth.

**WHAT is the difference between a man with no
tongue and a St Mirren fan?**
The man with no tongue has better taste.

WHAT'S the difference between Duncan Ferguson and
Marks & Spencer?
You always get a full refund on unwanted goods at
Marks & Spencer.

What's the difference between a
Celtic fan and a lemon?
One's yellow, bitter and twisted,
and the other's a citrus fruit!

WHY is the pitch at Fir Park so green?
Because they keep putting lots of crap on it.

**WHAT'S the difference between the Dundee bus and
a door?**
The Dundee bus has more knobs on it.

WHAT'S the difference between a Rangers fan and a
coconut?
One's thick and hairy, and the other grows on trees.

WALTER Smith goes into a building society to deposit some money. Whilst there, a robbery takes place, and the Everton boss is knocked unconscious in a struggle.

A few minutes later, Walter comes round but he is confused and mumbles: "What... how... er... where am I?"

"Relax. Your in the Nationwide," says a paramedic.

Smith says: "Bloody Hell! You mean I've been asleep all season?"

A 22-year-old secretary from Partick was on holiday in Australia. As she walked along Bondi Beach she could not help but notice all the other girls had huge breasts while she had a rather insignificant pair of jugs.

Suddenly, she spied a murky old bottle that had washed up on the beach. She had nothing else to do so she picked it up and opened the top,

Poof! Out emerged a genie, complete with flowing robes who offered to grant the two wishes she desired most.

"Then, give me the two biggest tits in the whole, world", she moaned.

Poof!! Poof!!

There before her eyes were Barry Ferguson and Paul Gascoigne!

DID you here about the Tory MP who was found dead in a Dundee strip? The police had to dress him up in women's underwear to save his family from the embarrassment.

THREE football fans were walking to a game when one noticed a foot sticking out of the bushes by the side of the road.

They stopped and after investigating, discovered a nude woman who had passed out with drink.

Out of respect and propriety, the Rangers fan took off his cap and placed it over her right breast. The Celtic fan took off his cap and placed it over her left breast.

Following their lead, the Aberdeen fan took off his cap and placed it over her crotch.

Then they called the police. When the officer arrived, he conducted his inspection.

First, he lifted up the Rangers cap, replaced it, and wrote down some notes. Next, he lifted the Celtic cap, replaced it, and wrote down some more notes.

The officer then lifted the Aberdeen cap, replaced it, then lifted it again, replaced it, lifted it a third time, and replaced it once more.

The Aberdeen fan was a bit upset and said to the cop: "What are you, a pervert or something? Why do you keep lifting and looking, lifting and looking?"

"Well," said the officer.

"I am just surprised. Normally when I look under an Aberdeen hat, I find a bum."

TOP TIP FOR DUNDEE UNITED FANS:
DON'T waste money on expensive new kits every season. Simply strap a large inflatable penis to your forehead, and everyone will immediately recognise which team you support.

THEY SAID IT!

"Their manager, Terry Neil, isn't here today, which suggests he is elsewhere." – **Brian Moore**

"With the very last kick of the game, Bobby McDonald scored with a header." – **Alan Parry**

"Well, it's Ipswich nil, Liverpool two. And if that's the way the score stays then you've got to fancy Liverpool to win." – **Peter Jones**

"You couldn't have counted the number of moves Alan Ball made … I counted four and possibly five.' – **John Motson**

"When one team scores early in the game, it often takes an early lead." – **Pat Marsden**

"And Meade had a hat-trick. He scored two goals." – **Richard Whitmore**

"I am a firm believer that if you score one goal, the other team have to score two to win." – **Howard Wilkinson**

"Ian Rush unleashed his left foot and it hit the back of the net." – **Mike England**

"It will be a shame if either side lose. And that applies to both sides." – **Jock Brown**

"He had an eternity to play that ball, but he took too long over it." – **Martin Tyler**

"Everything in our favour was against us." – **Danny Blanchflower**

"And so they have not been able to improve on their hundred percent record." – **Sports Roundup**

"Don't tell those coming in now the result of that fantastic match. Now let's have another look at Italy's winning goal."
– **David Coleman**

"Nearly all of the Brazilian players are wearing yellow shirts. It's a fabulous kaleidoscope of colour – John Motson

"Queen's Park against Forfar. You can't get more romantic than that." – **Archie MacPherson**

"Who can forget this fixture last year. 4-3 I think it was." – **Derek Johnstone**

"It looks as if Hearts have reverted to a five-man back four." – **Alan McInally**

A LIGHTNING strike simultaneously kills both Ian McGeechan and Clive Woodward. They ascend to heaven where God meets them and says: "Come in and I'll show you to your accommodation."

He takes Clive to a pretty cottage by a stream. There are lovely flower beds and the thatched roof forms a St George's cross. Birds are whistling Swing Low Sweet Chariot, and the gnomes by the garden path are images of English rugby heroes such as David Duckham, Wade Dooley and Bill Beaumont.

God then leads Ian McGeechan back up the path towards a grand mansion, with massive pillars, Scottish Lions on the gates, rolling lawns and fields of heather all around. Massive golden statues of Ken Scotland, Andy Irvine, Roy Laidlaw, Finlay Calder, John Jeffrey and Gavin Hastings overlook a magnificent display of prize flowers, spelling out the words Alba Siol Ghoraidh. Massed choirs of angels are singing Flower of Scotland.

Clive runs after God and Ian McGeechan, and says. "Excuse me, God, I'm honored by my wonderful new accommodation, and I don't wish to sound ungrateful, but I was wondering why Ian's house is so much bigger, and even more grand than mine."

God laughs, puts a consoling arm around Clive's shoulder, and says softly: "Don't worry Clive. That's not Ian's house. It's mine!"

WHY do Dundee fans plant seed potatoes behind the goal at Dens? So that they have something to lift at the end of the season.

BEFORE a recent Old Firm match, things got a bit
hairy between the fans. Bottles were thrown as rival
supporters made their way to the big game.

One young spectator, stuck in the middle, was naturally
concerned for his safety, so an old boy went to his side
and put his arm round his shoulder to reassure him.

"Don't worry, son," he said. "It's like bombs in the war.
One of those won't hit unless it's got your name on it."

"That's what worries me," said the youngster. "My name
is Johnny Walker."

FOOTBALL ANAGRAMS:

Alex Ferguson = Sex organ fuel
David Ginola = A livid gonad
Andy Gray = Randy Gay
Teddy Sheringham = He'd shag dirty men
Paul Merson = Lump on arse
Martin Keown = I'm not wanker
George Best = Go get beers
Fabrizio Ravanelli = Evil Brazilian afro
Dennis Bergkamp = Pink German beds

HAVE you heard about the new OXO cube launched by
Aberdeen boss Ebbe Skovdahl?

It's called Laughing Stock..

REPORT in a Scottish newspaper:

"Tannadice has been broken into and the entire contents
of the trophy room stolen. Police are believed to be
looking for a man with a tangerine carpet."

RUMOUR has it that St Johnstone have got a new sponsor: Tampax.
The board thought it was an appropriate change as the club is going through a very bad period.

HOW many Manchester United fans does it take to change a light bulb?
Three. One to change the bulb, one to buy the "2001 Lightbulb Changing" commorative tee-shirt and video, and one to drive the other two back to London.

A LITTLE boy from Glasgow had gone to Rome on holiday with his family hoping to see the Pope.
Anyway, a couple of days after they'd arrived the Pope was doing a tour of the city in his Popemobile.
The boy was worried the Pope wouldn't be able to pick him out in the crowd but his mum said: "Don't worry. The Pope is a footy fan. Wear your Celtic shirt and he's bound to pick you out and talk to you."
So, they're in the crowd but the Popemobile drives past them and stops further down the street where John Paul gets out and speaks to a little boy in a Rangers shirt.
The Glasgow lad is distraught and starts crying. His Mum says: "Don't worry, the Pope's driving around tomorrow as well so we'll get you an Rangers shirt and then he's bound to stop to see you."
The next day arrives and the boy has got on his new Rangers shirt.
The Popemobile stops right by him, John Paul gets out, bends down and says to the lad: "I thought I told you to piss off yesterday?"

Farce of the Law

Lawyers, don't ya just love them! My mate is a lawyer, but he keeps it quiet. He just tells people he plays the piano in a brothel.

HEAR about the kidnapper who hijacked a plane full of lawyers?
He threatened to release one every hour if his demands weren't met.

A LAWYER is standing in a queue when suddenly he feels a pair of hands kneading his back, and neck.
The lawyer turns around and yells: "What the hell do you think you're doing?"
The bloke behind him replies: "I'm a chiropractor and just keeping in practice while I'm waiting."
"Well, I'm a lawyer, but you don't see me screwing the guy in front of me, do you?"

HOW do you stop a lawyer from drowning?
Shoot him before he hits the water.

A MAN walks into a bar where he sees a beautiful, well-dressed woman sitting on a bar stool.
He walks up to her and says: "Hi there, how's it going?"
She turns to him, looks him straight in the eyes and says, "I'll screw anybody, any time, any where – your place or my place, it doesn't matter one iota."
The guy raises his eyebrows and says, "No shit! What firm of solicitors do you work for?"

WHAT do you have when 100 lawyers are buried up to their neck in sand?
Not enough sand.

A GUY walks into a post office one day to see a man at the counter methodically placing "Love" stamps on bright pink envelopes with hearts all over them.

He then takes out perfume and sprays scent all over them. As he watches this, the guy's curiosity gets the better of him and he asks the man what he's doing.

"I'm sending out 1,000 Valentine cards signed: "Guess who?""

"But why?" asks the man.

"I'm a divorce lawyer."

DID you hear about the new sushi bar that caters exclusively to lawyers? It's called, Sosumi.

HOW many lawyers does it take to roof a house? It all depends on how thinly you slice them up.

AN ELDERLY lawyer was on his death bed when he called to his wife.

He told her to run and get a Bible as soon as possible. Being a religious woman, she thought this was a good idea. She ran and got it, prepared to read him his favourite verse or something of the sort.

He snatched it from her and began quickly scanning pages, his eyes darting right and left.

The wife was curious, so she asked: "What are you doing?"

"I'm looking for loopholes!" he shouted.

A LAWYER married a woman who had previously divorced ten husbands. On their wedding night, she told her new husband: "Please be gentle, I'm a virgin."

"What?" said the puzzled groom. "How can that be if you've been married ten times?"

"Well, Husband No.1 was a sales representative. He kept telling me how great it was going to be.

"Husband No.2 was in computer support. He was said he'd look into it and get back to me.

"Husband No.3 was from field services. He said everything checked out diagnostically but he just couldn't get the system up.

"Husband No.4 was in telesales. Even though he knew he had the order, he didn't know when he would be able to deliver.

"Husband No.5 was an engineer. He understood the basic process but wanted three years to research and design a new state-of-the-art method.

"Husband No.6 was from administration. He thought he knew how, but wasn't sure if it was his job or not.

"Husband No.7 was in marketing. Although he had a nice product, he was never sure how to position it.

"Husband No.8 was a psychologist. All he ever did was talk about it.

"Husband No.9 was a gynecologist. All he did was look at it.

"Husband No.10 was a stamp collector. All he ever did was ... God! I miss him! But now that I've married you, I'm really excited!"

"Good," said the new husband, "but, why?"

"You're a lawyer. This time I know I'll get screwed!"

AN engineer dies and reports to the pearly gates. St Peter checks his dossier and says: "Ah, you're an engineer – you're in the wrong place."

So, the engineer reports to the gates of hell and is let in. Pretty soon, the engineer gets dissatisfied with the level of comfort in hell and starts designing improvements. After a while, they've got air conditioning, flush toilets and lifts, and the engineer is everybody's mate.

One day, God calls Satan up on the telephone and says with a sneer: "So, how's it going down there in hell?"

Satan replies: "Things are great. We've got flush toilets, air conditioning and lifts, and there's no telling what this engineer is going to come up with next."

God replies: "What? You've got an engineer? That's a mistake. He shouldn't be down there, send him back."

Satan says: "No way. I like having an engineer on the staff, and I'm keeping him."

God says, "Send him back up here or I'll sue."

Satan laughs uproariously and answers: "Yeah, right. And just where are YOU going to get a lawyer?"

A CLIENT phones his solicitors and says: "I want to speak to my lawyer."

The receptionist replies: "I'm sorry. He died last week."

The next day the guy phones again and asks for the lawyer only to be told again by the receptionist that his solicitor had passed away.

But the same guy phones back the next day asking for his lawyer. Exasperated and upset, the receptionist says: "This is third time I've told you your lawyer is dead. Why do you keep calling?"

The guy replies: "Because I love hearing it!"

WHAT'S the difference between a female lawyer and a pitbull? Lipstick.

A DOCTOR and a lawyer in separate vehicles collided on the Kingston Bridge one foggy night.

The fault was questionable, but both were shaken up, so the lawyer offered the doctor a drink from a hip flask.

The doctor took the flask with a shaking hand and belted back a couple of swallows.

As the lawyer started to put the cap back on the flask the doctor asked: "Aren't you going to have one too, for your nerves?"

"Of course I am," replied the lawyer. "After the police get here."

WHAT can a goose do that a duck can't but a lawyer should? Shove its bill up its ass!

A YOUNG couple were driving to Gretna Green to get married. On their way, however, they are involved in a freak car accident and both are killed.

They go to Heaven and at the Pearly Gates they meet St Peter. The couple tell the keeper of the gates they were on their way to get married when the accident happened, and they begged him to arrange it so they could marry in Heaven.

St Peter promised them that he'll do his best to work on it for them.

Three months pass by the couple hear nothing.

Then one day they bump into the saint and remind him about their hopes to tie the knot.

He says: "I'm still working on it."

Two years pass by and no marriage but St Peter again assures them he's working on it.

Finally after 20 long years St Peter comes running with a minister and tells the couple it's time for their wedding.

The couple marry and live happily for a while. But after a few months the couple decide things are not working out and ask St Peter to organise a divorce.

"Can you arrange it for us?" they ask.

St Peter replies: "Are you kidding? It took 20 years to find a priest up here. How am I gonna find a lawyer?"

A MAN walks into a Bellshill pub with a crocodile tucked under his arm and asks the barman: "Do you serve solicitors here?" "Sure do," says the barman eyeing up the croc. "Good," says the man. "Give me a beer and I'll have a lawyer for my crocodile."

***WHY does the Law Society prohibit solictors and
clients from having sex?
To prevent clients from being billed twice for
essentially the same service.***

A VERY successful lawyer parked his brand-new Lotus
in front of his office to show it off to his colleagues.
As he got out, a lorry passed too close and completely
tore off the door on the driver's side of his pride and
joy. The solicitor grabbed his mobile phone, called the
polis and within minutes a copper pulled up.
Before the officer had a chance to ask any questions, the
lawyer started screaming hysterically.
His Lotus, which he had just picked up the day before,
was completely ruined and would never be the same,
no matter what the body shop did to it.
When the lawyer finally calmed down, the officer shook
his head in disgust. He said: "I can't believe how
materialistic you lawyers are. You are so focused on
your possessions you don't notice anything else."
"How can you say such a thing?" asked the lawyer.
The cop replied: "Don't you know your left arm is
missing from the elbow down? It must have been torn
off when the truck hit you."
"Ahhh!" screamed the lawyer. "Where's my Rolex!"

A TEACHER, a thief and a lawyer all die in the same freak accident. When they reach Heaven, St Peter tells them that because of overcrowding, they each have to answer a question correctly to gain admission.

The teacher is first, and St Peter asks, "Name the famous ship that was sunk by an iceberg?"

"Phew, that one's easy," says the teacher, "The Titanic."

"Alright," said St.Peter, "you may pass."

Then the thief got his question: "How many died on the Titanic?"

The thief replied: "That's tough, but fortunately I saw the film. The answer is 1500 people."

And so he passed through.

Last, St Peter gave the lawyer his question: "Name them."

A LAWYER named Mr Strange was shopping for a headstone. After he had made his selection, the mason asked what inscription he would like on it.

"Here lies an honest man and a lawyer," responded the lawyer.

"Sorry, but I can't do that," replied the stonecutter. "It is against the law to bury two people in the same grave."

Mr Strange was not amused by this attempt at humour and asked if he had another suggestion.

The stonecutter said: "I could write 'Here lies an honest lawyer'."

The lawyer protested: "But that won't tell people who it was."

"It most certainly will," retorted the stonecutter. "People will read 'Here lies an honest lawyer' and exclaim, 'That's Strange!'"

A SOLICITOR was walking down the street and saw a
  dreadful car accident.
He rushed over, started handing out business cards and
  said: "I saw the whole thing. I'll take either side."

A BARBER gave a haircut to a priest one
  day. The priest tried to pay for the haircut
  but the barber refused saying: "I cannot
  accept money. You are a good man – you
  do God's work."
The next morning the barber found a dozen
  bibles at the door to his shop.
Then a policeman came for a trim, and
  again the barber refused payment. He said:
  "I cannot accept money from you. You are
  a good man – you protect the public."
The next morning the barber found a bag of
  sweeties at the door to his shop.
Next a lawyer came to the barber and again
  he refused payment saying: "I cannot
  accept money from you. You are a good
  man – you serve the justice system."
The next morning the barber found a dozen
  more lawyers waiting for a haircut.

A YOUNG boy walked up to his father and asked:
  "Dad? Does a lawyer ever tell the truth?"
The father thought for a moment. "Yes son," he replied.
  "A lawyer will do anything to win a case."

A BURGLAR hires a hot-shot lawyer known for his clever pleas in defence.

At the sheriff court, the solicitor tells the judge: "My client merely inserted his arm into the window and removed a few items. His arm is not himself and I fail to see how you can punish the whole individual for an offense committed by his limb."

"Well put," the judge replied. "Using your logic, I sentence your client's arm to a year in jail. He can accompany it or not, as he chooses."

The defendant smiled. With his lawyer's assistance he detached his false limb and walked free.

AFTER dozens of expensive tests and weeks in hospital, a rich old man is told he has only 24 hours to live.

The dying man called his two lawyers to his room and asked them to stand by either side of his bed.

After standing for some time, the first lawyer asked, "What do you want me to do?"

"Nothing. Just stand there."

A while later, the second lawyer asked the same question and was again told to stand still.

As the hours wore on, the man weakened and when he was on his last gasp, the lawyers asked again: "Why are we standing here?"

"Well," said the old man, "Christ died between two thieves. I thought I'd do the same!

AN OLD man was critically ill. Feeling that death was near, he called his lawyer.

"I want to become a lawyer," the dying man said. "How much is it for the express degree you told me about?"

"It's £50,000," the lawyer said. "But why? You'll be dead soon, why do you want to become a lawyer?"

"That's my business! Get me the course!"

Four days later, the old man got his law degree. His lawyer was at his bedside, making sure his bill would be paid.

Suddenly the old man was racked with coughs and it was clear the end was soon. Still curious, the lawyer asked: "Please, before it's too late. Tell me why you wanted to to get a law degree so badly before you died."

In a faint whisper, as he breathed his last, the old man said: "One less lawyer . . ."

TWO solicitors went into a cafe and ordered drinks.
Then they produced sandwiches from their briefcases and started to eat.

The owner became quite concerned and marched over and told them: "Hey, you can't stroll in here and eat your own sandwiches!"

The lawyers looked at each other, shrugged their shoulders – and then exchanged sandwiches.

IT was a nice day at the park by the lake. Three guys were casting their lines to catch some fish and a couple were rowing in a small boat.

Two crows were cruising by looking for targets to crap on. The younger of the two crows tried to show off and dive-bombed the fisherman.

Plop, plop, plop.

But the crap landed with a thud, thud – hitting only two of the three men.

The older crow aimed at the couple in the moving rowing boat.

Plop, plop.

And this time they landed with a single thud – hitting only one of the couples.

Then out from nowhere came this little bird, wings still wet like it was just been hatched. It swooped down at the three fishermen.

Plop, plop, plop. Thud, thud, thud.

It swooped over to the row boat.

Plop, plop. Thud, thud.

Then a kid riding a bike came around. It flew over there.

Plop. Thud.

And then the bird rested on a tree branch. The crows were impressed and went over, asking:

"Where do you learn to do that?"

The little bird said: "I might just be a baby bird but I've plenty of experience. In my former life I was a lawyer."

Do you know what happens when a lawyer takes Viagra? He becomes taller.

What's the definition of a tragedy? A bus full of lawyers crashes but one seat is empty.

A LAWYER was on holiday in a small farming town in
Angus. While walking through the streets, a tractor was
involved in an accident.

A large crowd gathered and instinctively the lawyer
wanted to get to the injured person, but couldn't get
near the car.

Being a clever sort, he started shouting loudly: "Let me
through! I'm the son of the victim."

The crowd made way for him. Lying in front of the car
was a sheep.

**AFTER years of hard work, Angie took her first
holiday on a luxury cruise ship.**

**While sitting in a deck chair, she recognised a long-
lost school pal so she crossed the deck, tapped her
on the shoulder and said: "Hello, Janet. I haven't
seen you in years. What are you doing these days?"**

**"I'm practicing law," whispered Angela. "But don't
tell my mum. She still thinks I'm a prostitute."**

A BUS load of lawyers were driving down a country road
when the coach went off the road and hit a tree in an
farmer's field.

The old farmer went over to investigate. He then dug a
hole and started to bury the lawyers.

A few days later, the polis came out, saw the crashed bus,
and then asked the old farmer: "Were they all dead?"

He replied: "Well, some of them said they weren't but
you know how them lawyers lie."

TWO lions are walking through the jungle when one of them reaches out with his tongue and licks the backside of the other.

Startled, his pal turns and yells: "Hey! Cut it out."

The lion apologises and they continue, but about five minutes later, it does it again.

This time, the offended animal banjoes the arse-licker and says: "I said stop it!"

But the lion won't take a telling and a few minutes later does it again. The front lion wheels round and finally asks what was wrong.

The rear lion replies: "Well, I just ate a lawyer and I'm trying to get the taste out of my mouth."

YOU'RE trapped in a room with a tiger, a rattlesnake and a lawyer. You have a gun with two bullets. What should you do? Shoot the lawyer. Twice.

A MAN visits his mate and notices his car is a write-off and covered with leaves, grass, dirt and blood.

He asks his friend: "What's happened to your car?"

"Well," the friend responses. "I knocked down a lawyer."

"OK," says the man. "That explains the blood. But what about the leaves, the grass, the branches and the dirt?"

"Well, I had to chase him through the park."

SOMEONE mistakenly left the cages open in the reptile house at Edinburgh Zoo and snakes were slithering all over the city.

Frantically, the keeper tries, but fails to get them back in their cages. Finally he says, "Quick, call a lawyer! "We need someone who speaks their language!"

A STINGY old lawyer had been diagnosed with terminal illness but was determined to prove wrong the saying, "You can't take it with you."

After much thought, the old ambulance chaser finally figured out how to take at least some of his money with him when he died.

He told his wife to withdraw all his cash from the bank and place it in two bags. These were to be left in the attic, directly above his bed.

His plan was to reach out and grab the bags when his spirit floated to Heaven.

Several weeks after the funeral, the deceased lawyer's wife, up in the attic cleaning, came upon the two forgotten pillow cases stuffed with cash.

"Oh, that old fool," she exclaimed. "I knew he should have had me put the money in the basement."

A CAR was badly damaged in a smash at a busy road junction and a good Samaritan rushed to see if anyone was hurt.

He saw the driver was dazed and bleeding: "Hang on there, lady," he said. "Are you badly hurt?"

"How the hell should I know?" she snapped. "I'm a doctor, not a lawyer."

WHAT'S the difference between a lawyer and a herd of buffalo?
The lawyer charges more.

WHAT is black and brown and looks good on a lawyer?
A Doberman.

WHAT do you call a lawyer who has gone bad?
An MP.

WHAT'S the difference between a dead dog in the road and a dead lawyer in the road?
There are skid marks in front of the dog.

HOW do you get a lawyer out of a tree?
Cut the rope.

WHAT'S the difference between a lawyer and a trampoline?
You take your boots off to jump on a trampoline.

WHAT do you call a lawyer with an I.Q of 40?
Your Honour.

A PETTY crook is sent to Hell for his sins. As he is being taken to a place of eternal torment, he passes a room where a lawyer was having an intimate conversation with a beautiful woman.

"What a joke," the man says. "I have to roast for eternity while a lawyer gets to spend it with a cracking burd."

Jabbing the man with his pitchfork, the Devil snarls: "Who are you to question that woman's punishment?"

TWO scientists were working late discussing ideas about behaviour modification studies.

"We've started something new at my laboratory," said the first scientist. "For some of our more dangerous experiments, we're now using lawyers".

"Lawyers?" asks the second scientist. "Why aren't you using rats?"

"Well you know how it is," the first scientist replies. "You can get attached to rats."

> **WHY don't sharks eat lawyers?**
> *It comes down to professional courtesy.*

THIS guy walks into a bar and shouts for all to hear: "Lawyers are ASSHOLES!"

A man in the back of the bar stood up and shouted back at him: "I take exception to that statement and I resent it greatly!"

The first guy said "Are you a lawyer?"

The man responded "No, I'm an asshole!"

IT WAS so cold last winter, I saw a lawyer with his hands in his own pockets!

WHEN a person assists a criminal in breaking the law before the criminal gets arrested, we call him an accomplice.

When a person assists a criminal in breaking the law after the criminal gets arrested, we call him a defence lawyer.

WHAT do lawyers use for birth control?
Their personalities.

A GANG of robbers breaks into a lawyer's club by mistake. The old legal eagles aren't daunted and fight back to defend their wallets.

In fact they put up such stout resistance, the gang was very happy to escape. "It ain't so bad," one crook noted. "We got £25 between us."

The boss screamed: "I warned you to stay clear of lawyers! We had £100 when we broke in!"

WHAT'S the difference between God and a lawyer?
God doesn't think He's a lawyer.

WHAT'S the difference between a lawyer and a carp?
One is a cold blooded bottom dwelling scavenger and
   the other is a fish.

DID you hear about Robby Knievel's newest stunt?
He'll attempt to jump 1,000 lawyers with a bulldozer.

A LAWYER'S wife dies. At the cemetery, people are
   appalled to see her headstone reads: "Here lies Phyllis,
   wife of Murray, L.L.D., Wills, Divorce, Malpractice."
Suddenly, Murray bursts into tears. His brother says:
   "You should cry. I can't believe a mistake like this has
   been made on your wife's headstone!"
Through his tears, Murray croaks: "You don't
   understand! They left out the phone number!"

A LAWYER was visiting a farmer on business, when he
   stepped out of his BMW and into a cow pat.
Looking down he cried, "My god I'm melting!"

HOW do you kill a lawyer when he's drinking?
Slam the toilet seat on his head.

WHAT'S the difference between a lawyer and a vulture?
Vultures wait until you're dead to rip your heart out.

Funny Bone

Laughter, they say, is the best medicine. In that case you are about to be cured of anything.

LITTLE Tommy is three and is just getting used to using the toilet. But when he goes to the bathroom, he manages to hit everything but the pan.

Every time his maw has to clean up after him. She is soon sick of it and carts Tommy off to the doctor.

After an examination, the doctor said: "His unit is too small. An old wives' tale is to give him two slices of toast each morning and his unit will grow so he can hold it and aim straight."

The next morning Tommy jumped out of bed and ran downstairs. On the kitchen table, are 12 slices of toast.

"Mum!" Tommy yells. "The doctor said I only had to eat two slices of toast."

"I know." said his mother. "The other ten are for your father."

A MAN is admitted to hospital with premature ejaculation. The doctors said it was touch and go.

THIS guy went to see a psychiatrist because he can't stop thinking about sex. The doctor showed his patient an ink blot and asked: "What does this remind you of?"

The guy replied: "A naked woman."

The shrink showed the man another inkblot and asked the same question. The guy responded: "A naked woman on a bed."

This went on and on, inkblot after inkblot. The psychiatrist finally said to the guy: "You are a sick pervert."

The guy replied, "I'm not the pervert here. You're the one who keeps showing me those dirty pictures."

What do Eskimos get from sitting on the ice too long?
Polaroids.

What do the letters "DNA" stand for?
National Dyslexics Association.

Why did the duck go to the doctor's office?
He was looking for a quack.

Why did the pilot go to the psychologist?
He thought he was plane crazy.

A joy rider lost his left arm and left leg in a car crash?
But he's all right now.

A WOMAN accompanied her husband to the doctor's for a check-up. Afterwards the doctor called the wife into his office alone.

He said: "Your husband is seriously ill. Unless you do exactly as I say he will be dead within weeks.

"Each morning, fix him a healthy breakfast. Be pleasant, and make sure he is in a good mood.

"For lunch and dinner make him a delicious, tasty meal. Then let him go to the pub and relax.

"Don't burden him with housework as he must not be subjected to stress.

"And most importantly, make love with him several times a week and satisfy his every whim.

"If you can do this, I think your husband will regain his health in a year."

On the way home, the husband asked: "What did the doctor say?"

"You're going to die."

AFTER years of misery a man visits his doctor to seek a cure for his severe speech impediment.

After a thorough examination, the doctor consulted with the patient and told him: "It appears the reason for your stuttering is that your penis is twelve inches long. Because of its size it is pulling on your vocal cords, causing you this annoying problem."

The patient replied: "Whhaaat cccan I dddo?"

The doctor scratches his forehead, thinks for a minute before revealing there was a surgical procedure which would ease the strain on the man's vocal cords.

This would involve removing six inches from the length of the penis to cure his stuttering.

Stuttering badly, the patient confides that his speech problems had caused him so much embarrassment. It had also caused him to lose his employment and made him shy with the ladies.

Anything would be worth a cure. So the doctor plans for the procedure. The operation is a success and six months later the patient comes in for his follow up.

Cured, he says: "Doctor, the operation was a success. I have not stuttered since the operation. I have a great new job and my self esteem is fantastic.

"However, there is one problem. My wife says she misses the great sex we used to have before the extra six inches were removed.

"So I was wondering if it is possible to re-attach those six inches which were cut off?"

The doctor scratched his forehead, thought for a minute and said: "I dddoonnn't ttthhhinkkkk thatttt wiiiilllll bbbbee posssssssibbble."

A VOLUPTUOUS woman went to see her gynecologist. The doctor took one look at her and his professionalism was a thing of the past.

Right away, he told her to undress and then started to stroke her thigh. As he did this, he said: "Do you know what I'm doing?"

"Yes," the girl replied said. "You are checking for any abrasions or dermatological abnormalities."

Next he began to fondle her breasts and asked: "Do you know what I'm doing now?"

"Yes." said the woman. "You are checking for lumps."

Driven by lust, the doctor ended up shagging his patient there on his examination table. He panted: "Do you know what I'm doing now?"

"Yes," she said. "You're getting herpes."

DID you hear about the prostitute who had to get her appendix out? The doctor sewed up the wrong hole and now she's making money on the side.

A SHORT-sighted surgeon was asked to operate on a patient who had a hopelessly gangrenous leg?

Unfortunately, the mixed-up medic amputated the patient's healthy leg by mistake.

Naturally, the patient sought compensation. Years of appeals came and went.

Finally, the High Court suggested the patient drop the case. Apparently he didn't have a leg to stand on.

AN ELDERLY man had an appointment to see a urologist who shared an office with several other doctors. The waiting room was filled with patients.

The old gent approached the receptionist, who was a large, imposing woman who looked like a wrestler, and gave her his name.

In a loud voice the receptionist said: "Yes, I see your appointment here. You want to see the doctor about impotence, right?"

The heads of the patients in the waiting room snapped around, to look at the very embarrassed man.

The old gent recovered quickly and in an equally loud voice replied: "No, I want a sex change operation. And, I'd like the same doctor that did yours!"

ONE DAY an old lady walked into the doctor's office. She said: "Doctor, I have a farting problem. I fart all the time. They don't smell and they are silent.

"In fact, I have farted 20 times since I entered this room and you didn't even know! Do you have a diagnosis?"

The doctor gave the little old lady some pills and sent her on her way.

The old woman came back to the doctor's office a week later, and said: "Doctor! What pills did you give me? Now when I fart, they stink!"

The doctor says: "Great. Now we've got your sinuses cleared up, let's work on your hearing."

"DOCTOR, doctor. Every time I stand up quickly, I see visions of Mickey Mouse, Donald Duck and Goofy."

"Ok, can you tell me how long you've ben having these Disney spells?"

A MAN tells his doctor that his wife has laryngitis. The doctor said there was nothing he could do to cure it.
The man said, "Cure it? I want to prolong it."

A HOSPITAL matron stopped a rather thick new nurse as she was going into the ward with a jug of boiling water.
"No, No! I told you to prick his boil!" she screamed.

A JELLY baby was feeling a bit under the weather so decided to visit his doctor.

The doctor checked over the jelly baby and decided to give him a blood test.

The doctor said: "Listen Mr Baby, I'm not sure what's wrong with you so I'll check the results of your bloodtest and give you a call tomorrow."

The next day the Jelly Baby received the call from the doctor.

"Hello Mr Baby. After looking at the results of your test, it seems that you have picked up a variety of sexually transmitted diseases.

Can I ask what you've been up to?"

"Well" said the jelly baby, "I've not been up to anything unusual. I've just been doing what any other jelly baby does."

"Ah!" said the doctor: "It all becomes clear now."

"You've been hanging around with All Sorts haven't you."

AFTER weeks of feeling unwell, a guy visits his doctor and has a full health screening.

Before his next visit, the GP is on the phone, sounding serious, and announces: "I'm afraid I've got some bad news and some even worse news. "

The poor guy is stunned but mumbles: "Well, you might as well give me the bad news first."

His doc said: "Your tests results are back from the lab and they reckon you only have 24 hours to live.

"24 hours! That's terrible! What could be worse?

The doctor replied: "I've been trying to reach you since yesterday."

JEFF was complaining to his pal Jack that sex with his wife was becoming routine and boring.

Jack, who was a bit of a stud, suggested: "Get creative. Why don't you try playing doctor and patient for an hour?

Jeff agreed: "Sounds great, but how do you make it last for an hour?"

Jack says: "Keep her in the waiting room for 55 minutes!"

A MAN was suffering from constipation so his doctor prescribed suppositories.

A week later, the man was back, complaining that the suppositories were useless.

The doctor says: "Have you been taking them regularly?"

"What do you think I've been doing," replied the man, "shoving them up my arse?"

A MAN has suffered all his life with severe migraine headaches. His consultant examines his history and carries out tests but discovers that his poor patient has had practically every therapy known to man for his migraines and STILL no improvement.

"Listen," says the doc. "I suffer migraines too and the advice I'm going to give isn't really anything I learned in medical school. This is what I have found helps, based on my own experience.

"When I have a migraine, I go home, get in a nice hot bath and soak for a while.

"Then I have my beautiful wife sponge me down with the hottest water I can stand – especially around the forehead. Sometimes she does it topless.

"This helps a little. Then I get out of the bath, take her into the bedroom and, even if my head is killing me, force myself to have sex.

"DOCTOR, doctor, I think I'm a kleptomaniac." "Try these" said the doctor, "And if they don't work, go and get me a DVD player."

"Almost always my headache disappears soon after. Give it a try and come back and see me in six weeks."

Six weeks later, the patient returns with a big grin on his face. he says: "Doctor, I took your advice and it works! It really works! I've had migraines for 17 years and this is the first time anyone has ever helped me!"

"Well", says the physician, "I'm glad I could help".

"By the way, Doc," the patient adds, "You have a really nice house."

Mr T from the A-Team is speeding down the road in the A-Team van. A little old lady crosses the road but Mr T sees her too late. He slams on the brakes and stops just inches from her but the aerials on the van whip forward, slashing her badly.

She's rushed to hospital where the doctor takes a careful look at her wounds and says: "This must be the worst case of van-aerial disease I've ever seen!"

How do deaf gynecologists work? They read lips.

A MAN goes to a doctor and says: "Doctor! Doctor! I have five penises!"

Astonished, the doctor says, "Good lord, man! How do your pants fit?"

"Like a glove!"

A doctor giving a circumcision told his patient: "Won't be long now."

A DOCTOR told his patient: "I've got good news and bad news Mr Smith. What do you want to hear first?"

"OK doc, tell me the bad news first"

"I'm afraid Mr Smith, that you'll never walk again."

"Christ! What the hell's the good news?"

"See that beautiful blonde nurse with the big tits?"

"Yeah"

"I'm taking her home tonight."

Blonde Faith

Thank God for dizzy blondes.
What would we do without
them. Or what would we do
WITH them... but that's another
story.

A BLONDE newly-wed calls her mum in tears. She sobs, "Robert doesn't appreciate what I do for him!"

"Now, now," her mother comforted, "I am sure it was all just a misunderstanding."

"No, mother," the young woman laments. "I bought a frozen turkey and he yelled at me about the price."

"Well, that's a bit mean," her mum agreed. "A frozen turkey isn't expensive – just a few quid."

"No, mum it wasn't the price of the turkey ... it was the airplane ticket."

"Airplane ticket? What did you need that for?"

"Well, when I went to cook it, I looked at the directions on the back. It said, 'Prepare from a Frozen State' so I flew to Alaska."

DID you hear about the blonde who got locked in the bathroom?
She was in there so long, she peed her pants.

A BLONDE, a brunette and a redhead were walking along Portobello beach when a seagull flew over and crapped all over the blonde making an awful mess.

The brunette says in a disgusted voice: "Hang on I'll nip to the public toilets just along the prom and get some toilet paper to wipe up."

After she leaves, the blonde begins to laugh.

The redhead says: "What's so funny?"

The blonde says: "Well, blondes are supposed to be so thick but look at her! By the time she gets back with that toilet paper the seagull will be miles away!"

BACK in the old Wild West, there were two blond cowboys, Wally and Dave.

One day, the two were enjoying a beer in the local saloon, when a man walked into the bar with an Indian's head under his arm.

The barman shakes his hand and says: "I hate Indians. Last week the bastards burnt my barn to the ground, raped my wife and killed my children."

He then says: "If any man brings me the head of an Indian, I'll give him one thousand bucks."

The two blonds looked at each other and walked out of the bar to go hunting for an Indian.

They wandered round for a while when suddenly they saw a Sioux brave. Wally threw a rock which hit the Indian square on the head.

The Indian fell off his horse and tumbled seventy feet down a ravine.

The cowboys made their way down the gully where Dave pulled out a knife to claim their trophy.

Suddenly, Wally said: "Dave, take a look at this."

Dave replied: "Not now, I'm busy."

Wally tugged him on the shoulder and says: "I really think you should look at this."

Dave said: "Look, you can see I'm busy. There's a thousand dollars in my hand."

But Wally was adamant: "Please, Dave, take a look at this."

So Dave looked up and saw that standing at the top of the ravine were five thousand red Indians.

Dave just shook his head and said, "Oh my God – we're going to be millionaires!"

A BLONDE hurries into the casualty ward late one night with the tip of her index finger shot off.

"How did this happen?" the doctor asked her.

"Well, I was trying to commit suicide," the blonde replied.

"What?" sputtered the doctor. "You tried to commit suicide by shooting your finger off?"

"No silly!" the blonde said. "First I put the gun to my chest but I thought, 'I've paid £6,000 for these breast implants, I'm not shooting myself in the chest'."

"So then?" asked the doctor.

"Then I put the gun in my mouth, and I thought 'I just paid £3000 to get my teeth straightened, I'm not shooting myself in the mouth'."

"So then?"

"Then I put the gun to my ear, and I thought, 'This is going to make a loud noise'. So I put my finger in the other ear before I pulled the trigger."

WHEN the employees of a restaurant attended a fire safety seminar, they watched a fireman demonstrate the proper way to operate an extinguisher.

"Pull the pin like a hand grenade," he explained, "then press the trigger to release the foam."

Later a blonde employee was selected to extinguish a controlled fire in the parking lot. In her nervousness, she forgot to pull the pin.

The fireman hinted: "Like a hand grenade, remember?"

In a burst of confidence she pulled the pin ... and hurled the extinguisher at the blaze.

Did you hear about the blonde who had a problem with her bed? She couldn't find a knife big enough to apply the bed spread.

WHAT'S the most effective way of keeping a blonde busy? Hand her a bottle of shampoo with the instructions: "Lather, rinse, and repeat."

What did the blonde's mother say when she asked if she could lick the bowl clean? "Just flush it like everybody else."

Why did the blonde take her typewriter to the doctor? She thought it was pregnant because it missed a period.

WHY did the American blonde have tyre marks on her back? She noticed a street sign which said "Don't Walk" so tried to crawl across the road.

THREE blondes are training to be detectives and are being tested in their skills of recognition. To do this, their instructor is showing each girl a picture for five seconds then quizzing them on it.

He shows the first blonde a picture, hides it then says: "This is your suspect. How would you recognise him?"

She answers: "Easy, he only has one eye."

The expert says: "Er, that's because the picture shows his profile."

Slightly flustered, he flashes the picture to the second blonde and asks her: "This is your suspect, how would you recognise him?"

The second blonde giggles, flips her hair and says: "He'd be too easy to catch because he only has one ear!"

The policeman angrily responds: "The picture only shows one eye and one ear because it shows the suspect in profile! Is that the best you can come up with?"

Next, he shows the picture to the third blonde and in a testy voice asks: "This is your suspect, how would you recognise him? And don't give me a stupid answer."

The blonde looks at the picture intently and says, "Hmmmm... the suspect wears contact lenses."

The policeman is surprised and says: "Well, that's an interesting answer. Wait here while I check and I'll get back to you."

He goes to his office, checks the suspect's file and finds out the suspect does in fact wear contact lenses.

He returns to the blondes and tells No.3: "Good work! How did make such an astute observation?"

"That's easy," the blonde replied. "He can't wear regular glasses because he only has one eye and one ear."

A CELTIC player drove his brand new Mercedes to his favourite sports shop and parked it outside while he went to do a little shopping.

After being in the shop five minutes a blonde salesgirl ran up to him yelling, "Excuse me sir, I just saw someone stealing your Mercedes!"

"Bugger! Did you try to stop him?"

"No," the blonde said. "I did better than that! I got the car registration number!"

NINE BLONDE INVENTIONS
1. The water-proof towel
2. Solar powered torch
3. A book on how to read
4. Inflatable dart board
5. A dictionary index
6. Ejector seat in a helicopter
7. Powdered water
8. Pedal-powered wheel chair
9. Water-proof tea bag

A MAN requested a blonde painter to paint him in the nude but she refused.

"I'll increase your fee two times," he said.

"No thanks!!" she replies.

"I'll give five times as much as you normally get!" the man states.

"Okay," said the blonde artist. "But you must let me wear my socks. I need somewhere to put my brushes."

WHY did the blond lay out on the lawn chair in her bikini at midnight?
She wanted to get a dark tan.

ONE night a blond nun was praying in her room when God appeared before her.

"My daughter, you have pleased me greatly," said God. "Your heart is full of love for your fellow creatures and your actions and prayers are always for the benefit of others. I appear now to thank and commend you, and grant you anything you wish."

"Dear Heavenly Father, I am perfectly happy. I am a bride of Christ. I am doing what I love. I lack for nothing material since the Church supports me. I am content in all ways," said the nun.

"There must be something you would have of me," said God.

"Well, there is one thing," she said. "It's those blonde jokes. They are so demeaning. I would like it if there were no more blonde jokes."

"Consider it done," said the Almighty. "Blonde jokes shall be stricken from the minds of human beings everywhere. But surely there is something that I could do just for you?"

"There is one thing," said the nun. "But it's really small, and not worth your time."

"Name it. Please," said God.

"It's these Smarties," said the blonde. "They're just so hard to peel."

A BLONDE girl in tears came running to her father who asked her what was the matter.

"You gave me some bad financial advice," she said.

Upset, her dad asked what it was.

"You told me to place all my money in a major financial institution and now that big bank is in trouble."

"What are you talking about?" said her dad. "It is one of the largest banks in the world. Surely there must be some mistake."

"I don't think so," said the blonde. "They just returned one of my cheques with a note saying, 'No Funds'."

FIFTEEN minutes into a flight from Glasgow to Paris, the captain announced: "Ladies and gentlemen, one of our engines has failed. Please don't worry. Our flight will be an hour longer than scheduled but we still have three engines left."

Thirty minutes later the captain announced: "Another engine has failed and the flight will take two hours extra. But don't worry. We still have two engines."

An hour later the captain announced: "One more engine has failed and our arrival will be delayed another three hours. We'll struggle on using our remaining engine."

A young blonde passenger turned to the man in the next seat and remarked: "If we lose one more engine, we'll be up here all day!"

A POLICEMAN saw a blonde down on her knees under a streetlight and asked if she was okay.

"I dropped my diamond ring and I'm looking for it," replied the blonde.

"Did you drop it right here?" asked the policeman.

"No," she responded: "I dropped it on the other side of the road but the light's better here."

A BLONDE and a redhead met for a drink and were watching the six o'clock news on TV. A man was threatening to jump from the Forth Road Bridge.

The blonde bet the redhead £50 he wouldn't jump and the redhead agreed.

Anyway, the nutter jumped and the blonde offered her pal the dough. The redhead said: "I can't take this, you're my friend."

The blonde said, "No, a bet's a bet."

So the redhead said: "Listen, I saw this incident on the five o'clock news. I can't take your money."

"Well, so did I, but I never thought he'd jump again!"

TWO telephone companies were putting up telephone poles across Rannoch Moor. At the end of the day, the company foreman asked the first crew how many poles they had put in the ground. "Fifteen" was the answer.

"Not bad, not bad at all," the foreman said.

Turning to the blond crew he asked how many they had put in. "Four" was the answer.

"Four?" the foreman yelled. "The others did fifteen yet you only did four?"

"Yes," replied the leader of the blond group, "But look at how much they left sticking out of the ground."

UNABLE to attend the funeral after his father died, a son who lived far away called his blond brother and told him: "Do something nice for Dad and send me the bill."

Later, he got a bill for £200, which he paid. The next month, he got another bill for £200, which he also paid, figuring it was some incidental expense.

But bills for £200 kept arriving every month. Finally the man called his blond brother again to find out what was going on.

"Well," said the blond. "You said to do something nice for Dad. So I rented him a Volvo."

IT WAS a hot, humid July afternoon when Susie, a blonde, decided to repaint her kitchen.

Instead of hiring a professional, she decided to do it herself. A friend thinking she might appreciate a break, brought over some cold juice and sandwiches.

When her friend arrived, he found Susie working hard painting the walls. But instead of wearing old clothes, she was wearing her fur coat and her ski parka.

He asked her why she was dressed that way on such a hot day. She brought him the paint bucket and told him to read the instructions.

He did. It said: "For best results, put on two coats."

★ ★ ★ ★

A BLOND, wanting to earn some money, decided to hire himself out as a handyman-type and started asking around a wealthy street.

He went to the door of the first mansion and asked the owner if he had any jobs.

The millionaire offer him £50 if he painted his porch. The guy agreed and the home owner dug out some paint and a set of ladders from his garage.

A short time later, the blond came to the door to collect his dosh.

"Finished already?" the man asked.

"Yes," the blond answered, "And I had paint left over so I gave it an extra coat."

Impressed, the man reached in his pocket for the £50.

"Oh and by the way," he said. "It's not a Porsche. It's a Ferrari."

A BLOND who had been unemployed for several months got a job with his local council. He was hired to paint white lines down the centre of a country road.

The foreman stressed he was on probation and had to complete the set average of two miles per day to remain employed. The blond agreed to the conditions and got down to work.

At the end of first day, the supervisor found that the blond had completed four miles – double the average! "Great," he said. "I think you're going to work out."

The next day, however, he was disappointed to find that the blond only accomplished two miles.

The supervisor thought, "Well he has still completed the average and I don't want to discourage him so I'll just keep quiet."

A BLONDE ordered a pizza and the cook asked if he should cut it in six or twelve pieces. "Six, please. I could never eat twelve pieces."

On the third day, however, the new recruit only painted one mile. The boss thought: "I need to talk to him before this gets worse."

The boss pulled the new employee in and says: "You were doing so great. The first day you did four miles, the second day two but yesterday you only did one mile. Why? Is there a problem?

"An injury? equipment failure? What's keeping you from meeting the two-mile minimum?"

The blond replied: "Well, each day I keep getting farther and farther away from the bucket."

JOHN gets a call from his blonde girlfriend, Sharon, who asks for his help.

"I've bought this jigsaw puzzle but it's too hard. None of the pieces fit and I can't find any edges," she tells him.

"What's the picture of?" asks John.

"It's of a big Rooster," replies Sharon.

"All right," says John. "I'll come over and have a look."

So he goes over to Sharon's house and she shows him the jigsaw. John looks then turns the blonde and says: "For Christ's sake ... put the cornflakes back in the box!"

WHY does a blonde keep empty beer bottles in her fridge?
They are for those who don't drink!

A BLONDE suspects her boyfriend of cheating on her so she goes out, buys a gun and arrives at his flat unexpectedly.

Sure enough, she finds him in the arms of a redhead. The blonde takes out the gun but is overcome with grief and instead puts the revolver to her head.

The boyfriend shouts: "No, don't do it!!"

"Shut up," she says. "The next bullet is for you."

WHAT do smart blondes and UFO's have in common?
You always hear about them but never see them.

A BRUNETTE, redhead and a blonde escape a burning building by climbing to the roof.

Firemen are on the street below, holding a blanket for them to jump into. They yell to the brunette: "Jump! Jump! It's your only chance to survive!"

The brunette jumps and SWISH! The firemen yank the blanket away. The brunette slams into the pavement like a tomato.

"C'mon! Jump! You gotta jump!" say the firemen to the redhead.

"Oh no! You're gonna pull the blanket away!" says the redhead.

"No! It's brunettes we can't stand! Redheads are okay."

"Right," says the redhead and she jumps.

SWISH! The firemen yank the blanket away and the redhead is flattened like a pancake.

Finally, the blonde steps to the edge of the roof.

Again, the firemen yell, "Jump! You have to jump!"

"No way! You're just gonna pull the blanket away!" yelled the blonde.

"You have to jump! We won't pull the blanket away!"

"Look," the blonde says, "Nothing you say is gonna convince me you're not gonna pull the blanket away!

So I want you to do is put the blanket down and back away from it . . ."

SANTA Claus, the Tooth Fairy, a dumb blonde, and a smart blonde are walking down a street when they spot a £100 note. Who picks it up?

The dumb blonde! Because, there is no such thing as Santa Claus, the tooth fairy, or a smart blonde.

111

A FAT blonde is put on a diet by her doctor who tells her: "I want you to eat regularly for two days, then skip a day, and repeat this procedure for two weeks."

When the blonde returns, she's lost nearly 20 pounds. "That's amazing!" the doctor says. "Did you follow my instructions?"

The blonde nods: "But I thought I was going to drop dead that third day."

"From hunger?" said the doctor.

"No, from skipping," replied the blonde.

**HOW do you sink a submarine full of blondes?
Knock on the door.**

A BLONDE was visiting Blackpool Pleasure Beach with friends. She found a drinks' machine, put in two coins, turned the knob and a can of lemonade fell out.

She picked up the can and put it in her pocket. Next she put two more coins into the slot and turned the knob. This time a coke fell out and she put it in her pocket.

This continued for a while and a man became curious about what she was up to. He said: "Excuse me Miss? What are you doing?"

She said: "Shhhhhh, can't you see I'm winning here!"

**WHAT goes blonde, brunette, blonde, brunette?
A blonde doing cartwheels.**

A BRUNETTE, redhead and blonde went to a fitness
  spa to relax. After lunch they visited the ladies room
  and found a strange woman sitting at the entrance.
She said: "Welcome to the ladies room. Our newest
  feature is a mirror which, if you look into it and say
  something truthful, you will be awarded with a wish.
"But if you say something false you will be sucked into
  the mirror to live in nothingness for all eternity!"
The brunette was first to approach the mirror. She said:
  "I am the most beautiful of us three." – And in an
  instant she was surrounded by a pile of money.
The redhead stepped up and said: "I am the most
  talented." – And she suddenly found the keys to a
  brand new Porsche in her hands.
Excited over the possibility of having a wish come true,
  the blonde looked into the mirror and said: "I think..."
  and was promptly sucked into the mirror.

*A BLOND walks into a hairdressers wearing a set of
  headphones. He sits down and asks for a trim.
The barber starts to cut his right side but stops and
  asks his customer to take off his headphones.
But the blond shouts: "I can't, I'll die!"
So the barber carefully cuts the right side, goes to the
  left side but again finds the headphones in the way.
He says: "You must take off your headphones."
Again the headphone man says: "I can't, I'll die!"
Enraged, the barber grabs the headphones and pulls
  them off. The blond chokes and falls down dead.
The barber picks up the headphones and listens.
  "Breathe In. Breathe Out. Breathe In. Breathe Out."*

BETTY and Bob have been back from their honeymoon for two weeks when Bob came home from work saying he'd invited four office friends for dinner that Friday.

Betty, being a blonde, is a bit apprehensive as she realises she must cook a meal for them all.

Bob explains there will be eight to cater for, as each pal would be bringing a spouse or date.

Since this is her first party, he consoles her by saying that all she has to do is order in some Chinese food and perhaps bake a cake. This sounds like a good idea and they sit down and decide what Chinese food to get.

Friday morning. Betty calls Bob's office in tears. She explains the only cake recipe she has is for six.

Her hubby says: "Why don't you just double the recipe?" She decides that is a good idea.

At 4pm, hubby gets another call – this time quite frantic. "I can't do it," his wife weeps. "It's impossible."

"Now, now, what's the matter?"

"Well, the recipe calls for two eggs."

"So, you use FOUR eggs. Don't you have them?"

"Yes. Then it needs four cups of flour."

"Well," Bob says rather testily. "You will have to use eight cups of flour – what is the problem?"

"It isn't the ingredients," Betty cries. "It says that the cake must be baked at 350 degrees and I have checked the oven and I can't turn the heat up to 700 degrees!"

WHY did the blonde have blisters on her lips?
She went around trying to blow out lightbulbs.

HOW did the blonde try to kill the bird?
She threw it off of a cliff.

HOW did the blonde break her leg raking leaves?
She fell out of the tree.

WHY did the blonde climb over the glass wall?
To see what was on the other side.

HOW does a blonde turn on the lights after having sex?
Opens the car door.

WHAT did the blonde say when she got pregnant?
"Gee, I hope it's mine."

WHAT'S the difference between a mosquito and a blonde?
When you slap a mosquito, it will stop sucking.

HOW did the blonde die while drinking milk?
The cow sat down!

A BLONDE, a brunette, and a redhead all work at the same office for a female boss who always goes home early.

"Hey, girls," says the brunette, "let's go home early tomorrow. She'll never know."

So the next day, they all leave right after the boss does. The brunette gets some extra gardening done, the redhead goes to a bar, and the blonde goes home to find her husband having sex with the female boss!

She quietly sneaks out of the house and returns at her normal time.

"That was fun," says the brunette. "We should do it again sometime."

"No way," says the blonde. "I almost got caught."

A WOMAN hired a contractor to repaint the interior of
her house. She escorted the handyman through her
home and told him what colours she wanted.

As they walked through the first room, the woman said,
"I think I would like this room in a nice cream."

The contractor wrote on his clipboard, walked to the
window, opened it and yelled out: "Green side up!"

He then closed the window and continued following the
woman to the next room.

The woman looked confused, but proceeded with her
tour: "In this room, I was thinking of an off-blue."

Again, the contractor wrote this down, went to the
window, opened it and yelled out: "Green side up!"

This baffled the woman, but she was reluctant to say
anything.

In the next room, the woman said she would like it
painted in a light rose. And once more, the handyman
opened the window and yelled: "Green side up!"

Struck with curiosity, the woman mustered up the nerve
to ask: "Why do you keep yelling 'Green side up' out
my window every time I tell you the colour I would
like the room?"

The contractor replied: "Because I have a crew of
blondes laying sod across the street."

How do you keep a blonde
busy? (see below)
How do you keep a blonde
busy? (see above)

117

A BLONDE reported for her University final exam which consists of "yes/no" type questions.

She takes her seat in the examination hall, stares at the question paper for five minutes then, in a fit of inspiration, takes her purse out, removes a coin and starts tossing the coin. She marks her answer sheet 'Yes' for Heads and 'No' for Tails.

Within half an hour she is finished while the rest of the class is sweating it out.

In the last few minutes, she is seen desperately throwing the coin, swearing and sweating. The moderator, alarmed, approaches her and asks what is going on.

"I finished the exam in half and hour. But I'm rechecking my answers."

A BLONDE was having problems selling her old car because it had 250,000 miles on the clock.

One day, she told a brunette pal the problem and she suggested: "I can maybe help you make the car easier to sell – but it's not legal."

"That doesn't matter," replied the blonde. "I want to sell the car no matter what."

"Okay," said the brunette. "Here is the address of my brother who owns a car repair shop. Tell him I sent you and he will turn the car's speedo back to 50,000 miles. Then it should not be easy to flog it."

The following weekend, the blonde made the trip to the mechanic and a month later, the brunette asked the blonde: "Did you sell your car?"

"No," replied the blonde. "Why should I? It only has 50,000 miles on it."

SALLY, a blonde, went into a wood with a package and a large bird cage.

She was gone several days and when she returned, her friend, Liz, had never seen her looking so sad so she asked her what was wrong.

Sally replied: "Because I just can't get a man."

Liz said: "Well, you sure won't find one in the woods."

"Don't be so silly," Sally said. "I know that. I went in the woods because I needed to catch a couple of owls. That's why I took a package of dead mice and a bird cage. But it didn't work!"

"How would owls help you get a man?" asked Liz.

Sally said: "Well, I heard the best way to get a man is to have a good pair of hooters."

WHAT do you call a blonde with half a brain?
Gifted.

A BLONDE is visiting London and wants to see round Buckingham Palace.

She asks a policeman for directions and the plod says: "Wait at this stop for the No.54 bus. It'll take you right there."

Three hours later the cop comes back and the blonde is still waiting at the same bus stop.

The policeman says: "Excuse me, but I told you to wait here for the No.54 bus. That was three hours ago. Why are you still waiting?"

The blonde says: "Don't worry, officer, it won't be long now. The 45th bus just went by!"

119

A BLOND, a brunette, and a redhead were trying out for a new NASA experiment on sending women to different planets.

First, they called in the brunette and asked her a question.

"If you could go to any planet, what planet would you want to go to and why?"

After pondering the question she answered: "I would like to go to Mars because it seems so interesting with all the recent news about possible extra terrestrial life on the planet."

They thanked her and said they would get back to her about her future role.

Next, the redhead entered the room and the NASA people asked her the same question.

In reply, she said: "I would like to go to Saturn to see all of its rings."

Again, the space boffins thanked her and said they would get back to her. Finally, the blonde entered the room and they asked her the same question they had asked the brunette and the redhead. She thought a bit and replied: "I'd like to go to the sun."

The people from NASA replied: "Don't you know that if you went to the sun you would burn to death?"

The blond smirked and put her hands on her hips. "Are you guys dumb? I'd go at night!"

A VENTRILOQUIST is touring the clubs and holds a show in a small venue in Lanarkshire.

With his dummy on his knee, he's going through his dumb blonde joke routine when a blonde in the fourth row stands starts shouting: "I've heard enough. What makes you think you can stereotype women that way?

"What does hair colour have to do with your worth as a person? Guys like you keep women like me from being respected and reaching our full potential."

The ventriloquist is embarrassed and starts to apologise, when the blonde yells: "You stay out of this pal! I'm talking to that little jerk on your knee!"

A SECRETARY is crying her eyes out at work one morning. Her boss notices and asks sympathetically: "What's the matter?"

The blonde replies: "I've just had a phone call saying my father has passed away."

The boss is very understanding and tells the young girl to take the rest of the day off and go home.

But the blonde claims she'd rather work to take her mind off the bad news. Later the boss checks on his secretary and is appalled to see she is hysterical. He rushes over and asks: "What's wrong now?"

The blonde says: "I've just spoken to my sister and her father has died too!"

A BLOND visits his doctor with a cucumber up his nose, a carrot stuck in his right ear, a banana in his left ear and an apple wedged up his ass. "What's wrong with me, doctor?" he asks. The doctor takes one glance and pronounces: "You're not eating properly."

INSTRUCTIONS FOR NEW CASH-POINTS

OUR new, drive-through cash-point machines will enable customers to withdraw money without leaving their cars. Please follow these instructions:

BRUNETTES:

1 Drive up to the cash machine.
2 Wind down car window.
3 Insert card into machine and enter PIN.
4 Enter amount of cash required and withdraw.
5 Retrieve card, cash and receipt.
6 Wind up window.
7 Drive off.

BLONDES

1 Drive up to the cash machine.
2 Reverse back to align car window with machine.
3 Restart stalled engine.
4 Wind down the window
5 Find handbag, remove all contents on to the passenger seat to locate card.
6 Attempt to insert card into machine.
7 Open car door to allow easier access to machine due to its excessive distance from the car.
8 Insert card.
9 Insert card right way up
10 Re-enter handbag to find diary with PIN written on the inside back page.
11 Enter PIN.
12 Press cancel and enter correct PIN.
13 Enter amount of cash required.
14 Retrieve cash and receipt.
15 Empty handbag again to locate purse.
16 Drive forwards two metres.
17 Reverse back to cash machine
18 Retrieve card.
19 Restart stalled engine and pull off.
21 Drive for three to four miles.
22 Stop to release hand brake.

Pet projects

Don't work with children and animals, they say. Well after reading this lot you'll understand why!

A MAN runs into the vet's carrying his dog and screaming for help. The vet lays the dog on a table and examines the still, limp body. After a few moments he tells the man that his dog, regrettably, is dead.

The man demands a second opinion, so the vet goes into the back room and comes out with a cat. He puts the cat down next to the dog.

The cat walks from head to tail poking and sniffing the dog's body and finally looks at the vet and meows. The vet looks at the man and says: "I'm sorry, but the cat thinks that your dog is dead, too."

The man is still unwilling to accept that his dog is dead, so the vet brings in a black labrador. The lab sniffs the body, walks from head to tail, and finally looks at the vet and barks. The vet looks at the man and says: "I'm sorry, but the lab thinks your dog is dead, too."

The man, finally resigned to the diagnosis, thanks the vet and asks how much he owes. The vet answers: "£550."

"What, £550 to tell me my dog is dead," exclaims the man!

"Well," the vet replies. "I would only have charged you £50 for my initial diagnosis. The additional £500 was for the cat scan and lab report."

TWO killer whales are swimming around the Arctic Ocean. One turns to the other and says: "See that fishing boat off in the distance? Let's swim over there, blow some water out of our blow holes, ram the boat and eat all the fishermen?"

The second killer whale answers: "Well, I am up for the blow job, but I don't swallow seamen."

SOME Indians capture a cowboy and bring him back to their camp to meet the chief. The chief says to the cowboy: "You going to die. But we sorry for you, so we give you one wish a day for three days. On sundown of third day, you die. What is first wish?"

The cowboy says: "I want to see my horse."

The Indians get his horse. The cowboy grabs the horse's ear and whispers something, then slaps the horse on the rump.

The horse takes off and two hours later it comes back with a naked blonde. She jumps off the horse and goes into the teepee with the cowboy.

The second day, the chief says: "What your wish today?"

The cowboy says: "I want to see my horse again."

The Indians bring him his horse. The cowboy leans over to the horse and whispers something in the horse's ear, then slaps it on the rump. Two hours later, the horse comes back with a naked redhead. She gets off and goes into the teepee with the cowboy.

The Indians shake their heads, figuring: "Typical white man – going to die tomorrow and can only think of one thing."

The last day comes, and the chief says: "This your last wish. What you want?"

The cowboy says: "I want to see my horse again."

The Indians bring him his horse. The cowboy grabs the horse by both ears, twists them hard and yells: "Read my lips! POSSE, damn it!

"P-O-S-S-E!!!!!"

A PANDA walks into a restaurant, sits down and orders a sandwich. He eats the sandwich, pulls out a gun and shoots the waiter dead.

As the panda stands up to leave, the manager shouts: "Hey! Where are you going? You just shot my waiter and you didn't pay for your sandwich!"

The panda yells back at the manager: "Hey man, I'm a PANDA! Look it up!"

The manager opens his dictionary and sees the following definition for panda: "A tree dwelling marsupial of Asian origin, characterized by distinct black and white colouring. Eats shoots and leaves."

THIS guy had a parrot he trained to sing. Once he took the parrot to the bar and told everyone that if you put a match under the parrot's right foot he would sing Jingle Bells and if you put the match under his left foot he would sign White Christmas.

Of course the people in the bar wanted to see it. And, sure enough, he put a match under the parrot's right foot and he sang Jingle Bells. He put the match under the parrot's left foot, and low and behold, he sang White Christmas.

One guy asked him what would happen if he put the match between the parrot's legs. He answered: "I don't know. Try it and find out."

So, the guy put a match between the parrot's legs, and immediately the parrot began singing: "Chestnuts roasting..."

TWO crayfish were in the fishtank in a posh seafood restaurant. The male crayfish made a pass at the female crayfish.
"Yes," she replied. "But will you still respect me in the mornay?"

A CITY type moves to the country and decides he wants to be a farmer. So he goes to the local farm shop and tells the man: "Give me 100 baby chickens."

The farm shop worker complies. A week later the man returns and says: "Give me 200 baby chickens."

Again, a week later the man returns. This time he says: "Give me 500 baby chickens."

"Wow," the arm shop worker replies. "You must really be doing well."

"Naw," says the man with a sigh. "I'm either planting them too deep or too far apart!"

TWO men are walking down the road and see a dog licking its balls. The first man says: "I wish I could do that."
The second man replies: "Better pat him first. He might bite."

THREE labradors – chocolate, yellow, and black – are sitting in the waiting room at the vet's surgery when they strike up a conversation.

The black lab turns to the chocolate one and says: "So why are you here?"

The chocolate lab replies: "I can't be house-trained. I pee on everything – the sofa, the carpet, the cat and the kids. But the final straw was last night when I pissed on my owner's bed."

The black lab says: "So what is the vet going to do?"

"Give me Prozac," answers the chocolate lab. "All the vets are prescribing it. It works for everything."

The black lab then turns to the yellow lab and asks: "Why are you here?"

The yellow lab says: "I'm a digger. I dig under fences, dig up flowers and trees, I dig just for the hell of it. When I'm inside, I dig up the carpets. But I went over the line last night when I dug a great big hole in my owner's couch."

"So what are they going to do to you," the black lab asks.

"Looks like Prozac for me too," the dejected yellow lab replies.

Then the yellow lab turns to the black lab and asks why he's at the surgery.

"I'm a humper," the black lab says. "I'll have sex with anything – the cat, a pillow, the table, anything. I want to shag everything I see. Yesterday, my owner had just got out of the shower and was bending down to dry her toes, and I just couldn't help myself I hopped on her back and started humping away."

The yellow and chocolate labs exchange a sad glance and say: "Prozac for you too, huh?"

The black lab says: "No, I'm in to get my nails clipped."

A LITTLE old lady walks into a taxidermist shop carrying the dead bodies of her pet male and female monkeys. She explains that they were her favorite pets and she misses seeing them around the house.

"Would you like to have them mounted?" asks the taxidermist. "Oh, no," she replies. "Standing side by side will be just fine."

AN old lady is rocking away the last of her days on her front porch, reflecting on her long life, when all of a sudden a fairy godmother appears in front of her and says she will be granted three wishes.

"Well," says the old lady, "I would like to be really rich."

*** *POOF* ***

Her rocking chair turns to solid gold.

"And, I wouldn't mind being a young, beautiful princess."

*** *POOF* ***

She turns into a beautiful young woman.

"Your third wish," asks the fairy godmother. Just then the old woman's cat wanders across the porch in front of them.

"Can you change him into a handsome prince," she asks.

*** *POOF* ***

There before her stands a young man more handsome than anyone could possibly imagine.

She stares at him, smitten. With a smile that makes her knees weak, he saunters across the porch and whispers in her ear: "Bet you're sorry you had me neutered."

A BEAR and a rabbit are walking through the woods when they see a golden frog. They are even more amazed when it talks to them.

The golden frog admits that he is a magical frog and doesn't often meet other residents of the forest, but when he does, he grants them three wishes each.

The bear immediately asks that all the other bears in the forest be female. The frog immediately grants this wish.

The rabbit, after thinking for a while, asks for a crash helmet and one appears, which he places on his head.

The bear is amazed at this, but carries on with his next wish. He asks that all the bears in the surrounding forests be female as well. This wish is also fulfilled.

The rabbit then wishes that he could have a motorcycle. It appears before him, and he climbs on board and starts revving the engine.

The bear cannot believe it. He remarks to the rabbit that he has wasted two wishes. Then, shaking his head, he makes his final wish: "I wish that all the other bears in the world be female as well."

The frog replies that it has been done and they both turn to the rabbit for his last wish.

The rabbit thinks for a second, then revs up the engine and drives off as fast as he can, shouting: "I wish for the bear to be gay!"

WHY are elephants grey? To distinguish them from blackberries.

A BURGLAR breaks into a house he thinks is empty. He tiptoes through the living room but suddenly freezes in his tracks when he hears a loud voice say: "Jesus is watching you!"

Silence returns to the house, so the burglar creeps forward again.

"Jesus is watching you," the voice booms once more.

The burglar stops dead again. He is frightened. Frantically, he looks all around. In a dark corner, he spots a bird cage containing a parrot.

He asks the parrot: "Was that you who said Jesus is watching me?"

"Yes,"says the parrot.

The burglar breathes a sigh of relief, and asked the parrot: "What's your name?"

"Clarence," said the bird.

"That's a stupid name for a parrot," sneers the burglar. "What idiot named you Clarence?"

The parrot says: "The same idiot who named the Rottweiller Jesus."

A MAN left his cat with his brother while he went on holiday. When he came back, the man called his brother to see when he could pick up the cat. The brother says: "I'm so sorry, but while you were away the cat died."

The man was very upset and yelled: "You could have broken the news to me better than that. When I called today, you could have said he was on the roof and wouldn't come down. Then when I called the next day, you could have said that he had fallen off and the vet was patching him up. Then when I called the third day, you could have said he had passed away. Anyway, how's Mum?"

"She's on the roof and won't come down."

WHY should you walk carefully when it's raining cats and dogs? You might step in a poodle.

A YOUNG blonde is on holiday in the depths of Louisiana. She wants a pair of genuine alligator shoes but won't pay the high prices in the local shops.

After becoming very frustrated with the "no haggle" attitude of one of the shopkeepers, the blonde says: "I'll just go out and catch my own alligator so I can get a pair of shoes at a reasonable price!"

The shopkeeper says: "Be my guest. Maybe you'll catch yourself a big one!"

Determined, the blonde heads for the swamps, set on catching herself an alligator.

Later in the day, the shopkeeper was driving home, when he spots the young woman standing waist deep in the water, shotgun in hand. Just then, he sees a huge alligator swimming quickly toward her. She takes aim, kills the creature, and with a great deal of effort hauls it on to the swamp bank.

Lying nearby are several more of the dead creatures. The shopkeeper watches in amazement as the blonde flips the alligator on its back.

Frustrated, she shouts out: "Damn it, this one isn't wearing any shoes either!"

WHAT do you call three rabbits in a row, hopping backwards simultaneously?
A receding hareline.

132

THREE bulls hear the farmer is bringing another bull onto the farm.

First Bull: "Boys, we all know I've been here five years. Once we settled our differences, we agreed on which 100 of the cows would be mine. Now, I don't know where this newcomer is going to get HIS cows but I'm not giving him any of mine."

Second Bull: "That pretty much says it for me, too. I've been here three years and have earned my right to the 50 cows we agreed are mine. I'll fight him, run him off or kill him – but I'm keeping all MY cows."

Third Bull: "I've only been here a year, and so far, you guys have only let me have 10 cows to take care of. I may not be as big as you fellows (yet) but I am young and virile, so I simply MUST keep all MY cows."

Just then a huge truck pulls into the yard and from it comes the biggest, most muscular bull they have ever seen. It is so heavy that it almost breaks the steel ramp with every step it takes.

First Bull: "Ahem... you know, it's actually been some time since I really felt I was doing all my cows justice. I think I can spare a few for our new friend."

Second Bull: "I have plenty of cows to take care of, if I just stay on the opposite end of the pasture from HIM. I'm certainly not looking for an argument."

They look at their young friend, the third bull, and find him pawing the dirt, shaking his horns, and snorting.

First Bull: "Son, let me give you some advice. Let him have some of your cows and live to tell about it."

Third Bull: "Hell, he can have ALL my cows. I'm just making sure he knows I'm a bull."

BILL'S all excited about his new rifle. So, he goes bear hunting in Alaska. The first bear he sees is a little brown bear and he kills it with his first shot.

There is a tap on his shoulder and he turns around to see a big black bear. The black bear says: "You've two choices. One, I maul you to death or two, we have sex."

Bill bends over for the bear. He's sore for two days, but he recovers and vows revenge. So he heads out on another trip to Alaska and he finds the black bear and kills him.

At that moment there is a tap on his shoulder. A huge grizzly is standing right behind him. The grizzly says: "That was a big mistake. You've got two choices. Either I maul you to death or we have sex."

Bill bends over. He survives, but he's really hurting and and he's outraged!

Sure enough, he heads back to Alaska and finds the grizzly and shoots him at point blank range. There's a tap on his shoulder. He turns around to find an enormous polar bear.

The polar bear says: "You don't really come here for the hunting, do you?"

ON a hot, dusty day a cowboy rides into a small frontier town. After dismounting, he walks behind his horse, lifts it's tail and kisses it where the sun don't shine.

An old man rocking by the general store witnessed the whole thing. "Whatya do that fer," he asks.

"Got chapped lips," the cowboy replies.

The old man asks: "Does that help?"

The cowboy says: "No, but it keeps me from licking them."

A TOURIST goes into a restaurant in a Spanish town for dinner and asks for the specialty of the house. When the dish arrives, he asks what kind of meat it contained.

"Senor, these are the cojones," the waiter replies. "They are the testicles of the bull killed in the ring today. They are the delicacy of our country."

The tourist gulps, but finds the dish to be delicious.

Returning the next evening, he asks for the same dish. After finishing the meal, the tourist commens to the waiter: "Today's cajones were much smaller than the ones I had yesterday."

"True, sir," said the waiter. "But you see, the bull, he does not always lose."

A YOUNG girl is walking in the park in the pouring rain when she sees three dogs. Being an animal lover, she starts to stroke one of them.

"You're lovely, aren't you," she says to the first dog. "What's your name?"

To her surprise, the dog answers her: "My name's Huey, and I've had a great day going in and out of puddles"

Delighted, she moves to the next dog. "And what's your name then?"

Again, unbelievably, the second dog answers her. "My name's Lewy, and I've had a great day going in and out of puddles."

And so she moves on to the last dog. "Let me guess," she says. "Your name's Dewy, and you've had a great day going in and out of puddles."

"No," replies the last dog. "My name's Puddles, and I've had an awful day."

REX the dog was sitting up in a seat at the cinema, excitedly barking at the on-screen hero and growling at the villain.

The man sitting behind said to the dog's owner: "That's incredible, I've never seen anything like it before."

"Yeah, he surprised me too," said the owner. "He hated the book."

A CAT dies and goes to heaven. There he meets the Lord Himself. The Lord says to the cat: "You lived a good life and if there is any way I can make your stay in Heaven more comfortable, please let me know."

The cat thinks for a moment and says: "Lord, all my life I have lived with a poor family and had to sleep on a hard wooden floor."

The Lord says: "Say no more." And a wonderful fluffy pillow appears.

A few days later six mice are killed in a tragic farming accident and go to heaven. The Lord is there to greet them with the same offer.

The mice answer: "All of our lives we have been chased. We have had to run from cats, dogs and even women with brooms. We are tired of running. Could we have roller skates so we don't have to run any more?"

The Lord says: "Say no more." And each mouse gets a beautiful pair of roller skates.

About a week later the Lord stops by to see the cat and finds him snoozing on the pillow. The Lord gently wakes the cat and asks: "How are you finding it here?"

The cat stretches and replies: "It is wonderful, better than I could have ever expected. And those meals on wheels you have been sending over are the best!"

A YOUNG boy was at the local shop to buy a big box of soap powder. The owner walked over and, trying to be friendly, asked the boy if he had a lot of laundry to do.

"Oh, no laundry," the boy said. "I'm going to wash my dog."

"But you shouldn't use this to wash your dog. It's very powerful and if you wash your dog in this, he'll get sick. In fact, it might even kill him."

But the boy was not to be stopped and carried the soap powder to the counter and paid for it, even as the owner still tried to talk him out of washing his dog.

About a week later the boy was back in the store to buy some sweets. The owner asked the boy how his dog was doing.

"Oh, he died," the boy said.

The owner said he was sorry the dog died but added: "I tried to tell you not to use that soap powder on your dog."

The boy replied: "I don't think it was the soap powder that killed him."

"Oh? What was it then?"

"I think it was the spin cycle."

A POLICEMAN was investigating a terrible car crash in
   which the driver and passenger had been killed. As he
   looked upon the wreckage a little monkey came out of
   the brush and hopped around the crashed car
The officer looked down at the monkey and said: "Boy,
   I wish you could talk."
The monkey looked up at the officer and nodded his
   head up and down and gave a little monkey yell.
"Can you understand what I'm saying?" asked the officer.
   Again, the monkey nodded his head up and made his
   noises.
"Well, did you see this?"
"Yes," motioned the monkey.
"What happened?"
The monkey pretended to have a can in his hand and
   turned it up to his mouth.
"Were they drinking?" asked the officer.
"Yes," the monkey nodded.
"What else?"
The monkey pinched his fingers together and held them
   to his mouth.
"Were they smoking a joint?"
"Yes."
"What else?"
The monkey motioned a sexual act.
"They were having sex, too?"
"Yes."
"Now wait a minute. You're saying your owners were
   drinking, smoking and having sex before they
   crashed?"
"Yes."
"What were you doing during all this?"
"Driving," motioned the monkey.

WEE Tommy was in the garden filling in a hole when his neighbour peered over the fence. Interested in what the youngster was up to, he politely asked: "What are you up to there, Tommy?"

"My goldfish died," he replied tearfully, without looking up, "and I've just buried him."

The neighbour was concerned. "That's an awfully big hole for a goldfish, isn't it?"

Tommy patted down the last heap of earth and replied: "That's because he's still inside your damn cat!"

A MAN goes into a seasfood restaurant and sees a sign that reads: "Big Red Lobster tails – £1."

Amazed at the value of the offer, he calls a waitress over.

"Excuse me," he said. "Is that sign correct?"

"Yes sir," she replied. "It's today's special offer."

"Fantastic," said the man. "But are you sure they're not small?"

"Oh no sir, I can assure you that they are very big."

"Are they out of date then?"

"No, no sir, they were brand new this morning."

"Well in that case, here's my £1. Fill me up"

The waitress took the £1 note, sat down beside him and said: "Once upon a time, there was a big red lobster..."

A DOG walks into a butcher's shop with a purse tied around his neck. He walks up to the counter and sits there until it's his turn to be served.

The butcher leans over the counter and asks the dog what it wants. The dog put his paw on the glass case in front of the mince, and the butcher says: "How many pounds?"

The dog barks twice, so the butcher makes a package of two pounds of mince.

"Anything else?"

The dog points to the pork chops, and the butcher asks: "How many?"

The dog barks four times, and the butcher makes up a package of four pork chops. The dog then walks around behind the counter, so the butcher can get at the purse. The butcher takes out the appropriate amount of money and ties the two packages of meat around the dog's neck.

A man who had been watching all this decides to follow the dog. It walks down the street and then trots up to a house where it scratches at the door to be let in.

As the owner appears at the door, the man says: "That's a really smart dog you have there."

The owner replies: "He's not all that smart. This is the second time this week that he's forgotten his key."

WHO did the stable owner summon when his thoroughbred horse was possessed by the devil?
An exhorsist.

EVERY night, Joe would go down to the off-licence, get
some bottles of beer and drink them while watching
telly.

One night, as he finished his last beer, the doorbell rang.
He stumbled to the door and found a six-foot cockroach
standing there. The cockroach grabbed him by the
collar and threw him across the room, then left.

The next night, after he finished his fourth beer, the
doorbell rang. He walked slowly to the door and found
the same six-foot cockroach standing there. It punched
him in the stomach, then left.

The next night, after he finished his first beer, the doorbell rang again. The same six-foot cockroach was there.

This time, Joe was kneed in the groin and hit behind the
ear as he doubled over in pain. Then the cockroach
left.

The fourth night Joe didn't drink at all. The doorbell
rang. The cockroach was back and it beat the snot out
of Joe and left him in a heap on the living room floor.

The following day Joe went to see his doctor and
explained the events of the previous four nights.

"What can I do?" he pleaded.

"Not much," the doctor replied. "There's just a nasty
bug going around."

141

THIS man owned a parrot which swore like a sailor. It could swear for five minutes straight without repeating itself. The trouble was the guy who owned him was a quiet, conservative type, and this bird's bad language was driving him crazy.

One day, it got to be too much, so the guy grabbed the bird by the throat, shook it really hard, and yelled: "Quit it." But this just made the bird mad and he swore more than ever.

So the owner got really mad and and locked the bird in a kitchen cabinet. This really aggravated the parrot and he clawed and scratched, and when the guy finally let him out, the bird cut loose with a stream of vulgarities that would make a veteran sailor blush.

At that point, the guy was so mad he threw the parrot into the freezer. For the first few seconds there was a terrible din. The bird kicked and clawed and thrashed. Then it suddenly became quiet.

At first the guy just waited, but then he started to think the parrot might be hurt. After a couple of minutes of silence, he became worried and opened up the freezer door.

The bird calmly climbed onto the man's outstretched arm and said: "Awfully sorry about the trouble I gave you. I'll do my best to improve my vocabulary from now on."

The man was astounded. He couldn't understand the transformation that had come over the parrot.

Then the parrot asked: "By the way, what did the chicken do?"

HOW are Tupperware containers and Walruses alike?
They both like a tight seal.

A LADY approaches a priest and tells him: "Father, I have a problem. I have these two talking female parrots, but they only know how to say one thing."

The priest asked: "What do they say?"

"They only know how to say: "Hi, we're prostitutes. Do you want to have some fun?"

"That's terrible," the priest exclaimed. "But I have a solution to your problem. Bring your two female parrots over to my house and I will put them with my two male parrots who I taught to pray and read the bible. My parrots will teach your parrots to stop saying that terrible phrase and your female parrots will learn to praise and worship."

"Thank you," the woman responded.

So the next day, the lady brings her female parrots to the priest's house. The priest's two male parrots are holding rosary beads and praying in their cage. The lady puts her female parrots in with the male parrots and the female parrots say: "Hi, we are prostitutes. Do you want to have some fun?"

One male parrot looks over at the other male parrot and exclaims: "Put the bibles away. Our prayers have been answered!"

WHAT do you call a deer with no eyes?
No idea.

A WEE girl asks her mum: "Can I take the dog for a walk around the block?"

Her mum says: "No, because the dog is in heat."

"What does that mean?" asks the child.

"Go and ask your father. I think he's in the garage."

The wee girl goes to the garage and says: "Dad, can I take the dog for a walk around the block. I asked mum but she said the dog was in heat and that I should ask you."

Her dad says: "Bring the dog over here." He takes a rag, soaks it with petrol, and scrubs the dog's behind with it. "Okay, you can go now but keep her on the lead and only go one time around the block."

The little girl leaves but returns a few minutes later without the dog.

Her dad says: "Where's the dog?"

The little girl says: "She ran out of petrol halfway down the street and there's another dog pushing her home."

A BLIND man walks into a department store, picks up his guide dog and proceeds to swing it about his head.

"Can I help you sir," asks a sales assistant.

"No, it's okay," the blind man replies. "I'm just having a look around."

144

Leftovers

Actually they were just too good
to leave out. There are some
really tasty morsels here.

JOE was successful in his career but as he got older he
suffered increasingly from terrible headaches. When his
personal hygiene and love life started to suffer, he
sought medical help.

After being referred from one specialist to another, he
finally came across a doctor who solved the problem.

"The good news is I can cure your headaches. The bad
news is that it will require castration. You have a very
rare condition that causes your testicles to press up
against the base of your spine. The pressure creates one
hell of a headache. The only way to relieve the pressure
is to remove the testicles."

Joe was shocked but decided he had no choice but to go
under the knife. When he left the hospital, his mind
was clear, and as he walked down the street he realised
that he felt like a different person.

He would make a new beginning and live a new life. He
walked past a men's clothing store and thought: "That's
what I need to cheer myself up – new clothes."

He entered the shop and told the salesman: "I'd like a
new suit."

The salesman eyed him briefly and said: "Let's see ... size
44 long."

Joe laughed: "That's right, how did you know?"

"It's my job."

He tried on the suit. It fitted perfectly. As Joe admired
himself in the mirror, the salesman asked: "How about
a new shirt?"

Joe thought for a moment and then said: "Okay."

The salesman eyed Joe and said: "Let's see ... 34 sleeve

146

and ... 16 round the neck."

Joe was surprised. "That's right, how did you know?"

"It's my job."

Joe tried on the shirt, and it fitted perfectly. As Joe adjusted the collar in the mirror, the salesman asked: "How about new shoes?"

Joe was on a roll and said: "Okay."

The salesman eyed Joe's feet and said: "Let's see ... size nine."

Joe was astonished. "That's right, how did you know?"

"It's my job."

Joe tried on the shoes and they fitted perfectly. He walked comfortably around the shop and the salesman asked: "How about a new hat?"

Without hesitating, Joe agreed.

The salesman eyed Joe's head and said: "Let's see ... seven and five eighths."

Joe was incredulous. "That's right, how did you know?"

"It's my job."

The hat fitted perfectly. Joe was feeling great, when the salesman asked: "How about some new underwear?"

Joe thought for a second and said: "Definitely."

The salesman stepped back, eyed Joe's waist and said: "Let's see ... size 36."

Joe laughed: "Wrong. I've worn size 34 since I was 18 years old."

The salesman shook his head and said: "You can't wear a size 34. It would press your testicles up against the base of your spine and give you one hell of a headache!"

A SCHOOLTEACHER asks his class: "Who can tell me which organ of the human body expands to 10 times its usual size when stimulated?"

Nobody raises a hand, so he calls on the first student to look his way.

"Mary, can you tell me which organ of the human body expands to 10 times its usual size when stimulated?"

Mary stands up, blushing furiously. "Sir, how dare you ask such a question? I'm going to complain to my parents, who will complain to the headmaster, who will have you fired!"

The teacher is shocked by Mary's reaction, but he asks the class the question again. This time Sam raises his hand and answers: "Sir, the correct answer is the iris of the human eye."

"Very good, Sam. Thank you."

The teacher then turns to Mary and says: "Mary, I have three things to tell you. First, it's clear that you have NOT done your homework. Second, you have a dirty mind. And third, I fear one day you are going to be sadly disappointed."

A POLICEMAN pulls over a car which is being driven
  erratically. He notices the driver is a priest and says:
  "You appear to have been drinking!"
The driver answers: "No officer, I am just tired."
The policeman sees an empty bottle on the floor and
  asks: "What is, or should I say was, in this bottle?"
The priest answers: "Water!"
The policeman sniffs the empty bottle and says: "It is
  not, it's wine!"
The priest looks up to the heavens and says: "Oh
  Lord, you have done it again!"

WEE Jimmy was hopping up and down bursting for the
  toilet.
"I wanna piss, I wanna piss," he cried to his mum in
  front of some of her friends.
Mum took him aside and gave him a row, saying that
  next time he needed the toilet, he shouldn't use that
  word but say something else.
Later that night wee Jimmy ran to his mum shouting: "I
  wanna whisper, I wanna whisper!"
His mum knew what he ment and took him to the toilet,
  after which she gave him a chocolate bar for not swearing.
That night the urge came over Jimmy again. He leapt
  out of bed and ran to his dad.
"What is it son," his dad asked.
"I wanna whisper, I wanna whisper Daddy!"
"OK son, come here and whisper in my ear."

ON the night of the school dance, a girl is changing upstairs while her boyfriend waits in the living room with her grandfather and her dog, Rover.

The boyfriend is nervous and thinks to himself: "I need a fart. I think I will let a little out."

So he does and the granpa yells: "ROVER!'"

The boy thinks to himself: "All right, now he thinks it's the dog. I will let a little more out."

So he does and the granpa yells again: "ROVER!"

The boyfriend says to himself: "Good, now he really does think it's the dog. I will let the rest out."

So he lets it rip and the granpa yells: "Rover, get over here before that guy craps on you!"

TWO detectives respond to a crime scene at a grocery store. One says: "What happened?"

The other answers: "Male, about twenty-five, covered in Bran Flakes and dead as a doornail."

"Good grief," says the first officer. "Didn't we have one covered in Corn Flakes yesterday? And another covered in Sugar Puffs last week?"

"You're right," said his partner. "This is the work of a cereal killer."

A CHICKEN and an egg are lying in bed, both sweating and breathing heavily.

They turn away and lie back. The egg looks to the bedside table, leans over and grabs a cigarette. The egg lights the cigarette and takes a deep puff.

It then turns to the chicken and says: "Well, I guess we know the answer to THAT question..."

OLD Jimmy had been a faithful Christian and was in the hospital, near death. The family called their local minister to stand with them.

As the minister stood next to the bed, Old Jimmy's condition appeared to deteriorate and he motioned frantically for something to write on.

The minister handed him a pen and a piece of paper, and Old Jimmy used his last bit of energy to scribble a note, then he died.

The minister thought it best not to look at the note at that time, so he placed it in his jacket pocket.

At the funeral, as he was finishing the eulogy, he realised he was wearing the same jacket that he had on the day Old Jimmy died.

He said to the mourners: "You know, Old Jimmy handed me a note just before he died. I haven't looked at it, but knowing Jimmy, I'm sure there's a word of inspiration there for us all."

He opened the note, and read: "Idiot, you're standing on my oxygen tube!"

A MAN walks into a fast food restaurant and orders a hamburger. As he waits for his food, he notices the cook is flattening the raw burgers by placing them under his armpits and squeezing.

He calls the manager over and points out what the cook is doing.

The manager replies: "Oh, that's nothing. You should see how he prepares the donuts!"

WHAT did Bill Clinton say to Hillary Clinton after having sex?
I will be home in 20 minutes dear.

STEVEN SPIELBERG, Arnold Schwarzenegger, and Pierce Brosnan are in the jungle shooting a movie.

Unfortunately, they are captured by fierce natives. As they are about to be executed they plead to the queen of the tribe for mercy.

She says: "Right. Get me something good to eat. If I like it, you will be freed."

The three stars agree and go into the jungle to look for some food.

Spielberg is the first to come back. He goes up to the altar and offers grapes. The queen tastes one and immediately spits it out. She orders her servants to shove the rest of them up his backside. The servants finish their duty, leaving a screaming Spielberg.

Schwarzenegger is the next to arrive with some yummy apples. The same thing happens to him, but curiously he laughs as the apples are inserted.

Spielberg is shocked. Here he is howling in pain with grapes up his backside yet Schwarzenegger with several apples up his is still laughing.

He asks: "What the hell are you laughing at?"

Schwarzenegger replies: "I've just seen Pierce coming back with a watermelon."

A MAN with a fifty-inch penis goes to the doctor complaining he can't get any women. The doctor says: "Well, I can't help you, but I know a witchdoctor who can."

So the man goes to the witchdoctor, who tells him to go to the lake. There he will see a magic frog. All he has to do is ask the frog to marry him. When the frog says "no", his penis will shrink ten inches.

So, the man goes to the lake and sees the frog. "Frog," he says, "will you marry me?"

"No," says the frog.

Suddenly, the man's penis is only forty inches long.

"That's good," thinks the man but I need it shorter.

Once again he asks the frog to marry him and when it says "no" his penis shrinks another ten inches. Now he is down to thirty inches.

"That's pretty good," he thinks, "but it could be a little shorter." So again the man asks the frog to marry him.

In a furious rage the frog answers: "For the last time! NO! NO! NO!"

AN ENGLISHMAN, an Irishman and a Scotsman were in a pub, talking about their children.

"My son was born on St George's Day," commented the Englishman. "So we decided to call him George."

"That's a real coincidence," remarked the Scot. "My son was born on St Andrew's Day, so we named him Andrew."

"That's incredible, what a coincidence," said the Irishman. "Exactly the same thing happened with my son Pancake."

A BOY is watching television and hears the name Jesus
   Christ. Wondering who Jesus Christ is, he asks his
   mother. She tells him that she is busy, and to ask his
   father. His father is also busy so he asks his brother.
   His brother kicks him out of the room because he
   doesn't have time to answer his stupid questions.
So the boy walks into town and sees a tramp in an alley.
He asks the tramp: "Who is Jesus Christ?"
The tramp replies: "I am."
The boy, not believing the tramp, asks for proof. So the
   tramp takes the boy into the bar down the street.
They walk up to the bar and the barman exclaims: "Jesus
   Christ, not you again!"

**WHAT do you say to a
one-legged hitch-hiker?
Hop in!**

A PASSENGER taps the taxi driver on the shoulder to
   ask him a question. Suddenly the driver screams, loses
   control of the vehicle, nearly hits a bus, mounts the
   pavement, and stops inches from a shop window.
For a second, everything is quiet in the cab, then the
   driver says: "Don't ever do that again. You scared the
   daylights out of me!"
The passenger apologises and says he didn't realise that a
   little tap could scare someone so much.
The driver replies: "Sorry, it's not really your fault. Today
   is my first day as a taxi driver – for the last 25 years
   I've been driving a hearse."

WHERE does Saddam Hussein keep his CDs?
In a rack.

A YOUNG man had been shipwrecked on a desert island for a couple of years when one day a beautiful woman emerged from the water. She was wearing a wetsuit which showed off her curves to perfection.

She wandered over to where the young man was sitting, sat down beside him and whispered in his ear: "Would you like a cigarette?"

"I haven't had a ciggie for years," he said. "Go on then."

She unzipped a pocket in her wetsuit, pulled out a pack of cigarettes, drew one out, lit it and handed it to the man."

She then whispered in his ear: "I'll bet you would like an ice cold beer too?"

"Oh baby, yes please," he cried.

She unzipped another pocket, took out a bottle of ice cold beer, opened it and poured some of it into a glass before handing it over.

She then moved even closer to him, nibbled his ear and said: "You fancy playing around?"

"Oh my God," he said excitedly. "Don't tell me you've got a set of golf clubs in there too!"

WHAT'S got 75 balls and screws old ladies?
Bingo.

THESE three French Foreign Legionnaires are walking through the desert under a baking sun. They're fully equipped with enough water for days and food aplenty.

On the shimmering horizon, mirages come and go and come again. They see visions of swimming pools attended by dusky maidens and stalls full of ice creams and sorbets of every conceivable flavour.

But the Legionnaires do not crack. Instead they keep marching solidly on.

Suddenly one of them freezes. "Psssst," he says. His companions halt and strain their eyes to where the first Legionnaire is pointing.

"Voila," he says. "Regardez, mes amis, isn't zat a bacon tree on ze 'orizon?"

And sure enough, there it is, proud and defiant in the middle of the desert, a bacon tree. Slowly they creep forward towards the far-off mystery object. Inch by inch, centimetre by centimetre, until they are within a stone's throw of the bacon tree.

Ever nearer they creep until suddenly a shot rings out, dropping one of the Legionnaires in his tracks.

The others hit the ground as bullets thud into the sand all around them.

The other two return fire and give first aid to their wounded companion.

Even as they bandage him and pour water over his face they can hear his faint voice.

"Zat was no bacon tree," he gasps. "Zat was an 'am bush."

POLICE were called to a Pizza Hut in Glasgow at the weekend after the body of a worker was found covered in mushrooms, onions, ham and cheese.
A police spokesman said that the cause of death had not been established but there was a strong possibility that the man had topped himself.

A WOMAN walks up to a old man rocking in a chair in his front garden.

"I couldn't help noticing how happy you look," she says. "What's your secret for a long happy life?"

"I smoke three packets of cigarettes a day," he said. "I also do a gramme of cocaine a day, a spliff of marijuana every night, a case of whisky a week, eat junk food, never exercise and do pills at the weekend."

"That's amazing," said the woman. "How old are you?"

"Twenty-six."

ONE day Dracula is walking down the street when suddenly a 10-ton load of smoked salmon sandwiches, sausage rolls, vol-au-vents, chicken wings, chipolatas, tomato salad, pizza slices and crisps descends on him from a great height and knocks him to the ground.

"Oh no," he gasps with his dying breath ...

"It's Buffet the Vampire Slayer!"

A COUPLE are watching Who Wants To Be a
   Millionaire, when the husband winks and says to his
   wife: "Let's go upstairs..."
She refuses, so the husband asks again. Again she says "no".
So the husband says: "Is that your final answer?" The
   wife says that it is.
So the husband says: "Well, can I phone a friend?"

**A LITTLE girl is puzzled about her origins. "How
   did I get here, mummy," she asks.**
**Her mother replies, using a well-worn phrase: "God
   sent you, sweetheart."**
"And did God send you too, mummy," she continues.
"Yes, sweetheart, he did."
**"And daddy, and grandpa and granny, and their
   mums and dads, too?"**
"Yes, dear, all of them, too."
**The child shakes her head in disbelief. "Then you're
   telling me there's been no sex in this family for over
   200 years?**
"No wonder everyone is so grumpy!"

A MAN is working at a chemist's and is always getting
   the prescriptions wrong. His boss tells him if he screws
   up one more time, he'll be fired.
One day an old man walks in and orders cough syrup.
   The assistant can't find any so he gives him a laxative
   instead. The OAP takes the laxative and leaves the
   store. The boss comes up and asks the worker why he
   gave the man a laxative in place of cough syrup.
He points towards the old man, who is suddenly leaning
   on a lightpost, and says: "Look at him. He's too afraid
   to cough now."

THREE men are at the FBI headquarters for a job interview. The head FBI agent tells the first man: "To be in the FBI you must be loyal, dedicated, and give us your all. Your wife is in the next room. I want you to go in there and shoot her with this gun."

The man takes the gun, hesitates, and says: "Sorry, I can't do it."

The next interviewee enters the office and the agent tells him the same thing he told the first guy. The second man takes the gun, walks into the room and walks out. "Sorry, I can't." he says.

The last man enters the office and the interviewer yet again explains the test. The man takes the gun and goes into the room. The agent hears six shots, silence, then a lot of screaming.

The man comes out of the room and says: "Someone loaded the gun with blanks so I beat her to death with the curtain pole!"

AN ENGLISHMAN, a Frenchman and an Irishman were discussing families. Amazingly it turned out that they all had 14-year-old daughters.

The Englishman said he had found cigarette butts under his daughter's bed. "I didn't know she smoked," was his lament.

The Frenchman then proclaimed that he had found vodka bottles under his child's bed. "I was not aware that she drank," he moaned.

The Irishman was adamant that he had the more pressing problem – he had found condoms under his daughter's bed. "I didn't know she was a man," he cried.

A GUY walks into a chemist's store and says: "I'd like some deodorant please."
"Aerosol?"
"No, under-arm."

FOUR guys are flying to Japan in a private jet. One is a Texan, one is a Mexican, one is a Frenchman and the other is an Englishman.

Suddenly the pilot announces that they must throw out all the luggage because there is too much weight to land. So they do.

Then they get another message saying three men will have to jump out because there is still too much weight.

The Frenchman goes to the door, shouts: "Viva La France," and he jumps out.

The Englishman goes next, shouting: "Long live the Queen," and he jumps out.

Next the Texan and the Mexican go to the door. They look at each other then the Texan grabs the Mexican and throws him out the door, yelling: "Remember the Alamo!"

WHAT did the egg say to the boiling water?
"How do you expect me to get hard? I just got laid five minutes ago!"

A FRENCHMAN and an Italian were sitting next to an Scotsman on an overseas flight. After a few cocktails, the men began discussing their home lives.

"Last night I made love to my wife four times," the Frenchman bragged. "And this morning she made me delicious crepes and she told me how much she adored me."

"Ah, last night I made love to my wife six times," the Italian responded. "And this morning she made me a wonderful omelette and told me she could never love another man."

When the Scotsman remained silent, the Frenchman smugly asked: "And how many times did you make love to your wife last night?"

"Once," he replied.

"Only once?" the Italian arrogantly snorted. "And what did she say to you this morning?"

"Don't stop."

A CITY boy is visiting the country and wants to go hunting. The farmer lends him a gun and tells him not to kill any farm animals.

The city boy heads off and soon after sees a goat. He creeps into range and finally shoots it. Not knowing anything about animals, the boy didn't know what he'd killed so he runs to the farmhouse and describes his kill to the farmer.

"It had two saggy tits, a beard, a hard head and it smelled awful," said the boy.

"Oh no," cries the farmer. "You've shot my wife!"

A MIDDLE-AGED American woman wants a husband but she is only willing to marry a man who has never made love to a woman before.

After several unsuccessful years of searching, she decides to take out a personal ad. She ends up corresponding with a man who has lived his entire life in the Australian Outback. And after a long-distance courtship, they decide to get married.

On their wedding night, she goes into the bathroom to prepare but when she returns to the bedroom she finds her new husband standing in the middle of the room, naked and all the furniture piled in one corner.

"What happened," she asks.

"I've never been with a woman," he says. "But if it's anything like a kangaroo I'm gonna need all the room I can get!"

HEAVEN was getting a bit crowded, so Peter began giving quizzes to see who should get in. A man came to the gates and Peter asked: "Who was the first man?"

"Adam."

"That's correct. Enter."

Another man came along.

"Where did Adam and Eve live?"

"Eden."

"That's correct. Enter."

Then Mother Theresa came along. Peter said: "I'll have to give you a difficult question. What did Eve say when she met Adam for the first time?"

"Mmm, that IS a hard one."

"Enter."

NICK'S been a hard-living journalist all his workin life but he decides to retire and get away from the hurly-burly. So he buys a small farm in the Australian Outback, as far from humanity as possible.

After six months of total isolation, someone knocks on his door. He opens it and standing there is a big, bearded Aussie.

"Name's Jim," says the Aussie. "I'm your neighbour from 10 miles over the ridge. Having a party Saturday and thought you'd like to come."

"Great," says Nick. "After six months of this I'm ready to meet some locals. Thanks for inviting me!"

Jim adds: "Gotta warn you, there's gonna be some hard drinking."

"Not a problem," says Nick. "I can drink with the best of them."

"Likely gonna be some fightin' too," continues the bearded Aussie.

Tough crowd, Nick thinks to himself. "Well, I get along with most people. Don't worry, I'll be there. Thanks again!"

Jim turns from the door, then adds: "I've seen some wild sex at these parties, too."

"Now that's not a problem," says Nick. "Remember I've been alone for six months! I'll definitely be there. By the way, what should I wear?"

"Whatever you want", says Jim. "There's just gonna be the two of us."

163

STEVE, Bob and Jeff are working on a very high scaffolding. Suddenly, Steve falls off and is killed. After the ambulance leaves with Steve's body, Bob and Jeff realise they'll have to tell his wife.

Bob says he's good at this sort of sensitive stuff, so he volunteers to do the job. After two hours he returns, carrying a bottle of whisky.

"Did you tell her," asks Jeff.

"Aye," replies Bob.

"Where did you get the bottle of whisky."

Bob says: "She gave it to me."

"WHAT," exclaims Jeff. "You just told her her husband died and she gave you a bottle of whisky."

"Aye."

"How come," asks Jeff.

"Well," Bob continues, "when she answered the door, I asked if she was Steve's widow? She said, 'No, no, you're mistaken, I'm not a widow!'

"So I bet her a bottle of whisky that she was."

GEORGE W BUSH and Vice-President Dick Cheney are at a restaurant for lunch. The waitress comes over and asks what they will be having.

Dubya says: "I'll have a quickie."

The waitress steps back in disgust and says: "Mr President, I thought that kind of behavior went out with the last administration!"

She storms off and Dubya looks confused. Cheney shakes his head at the President and says: "George, it's pronounced QUICHE."

A DEPRESSED young woman was so desperate that she decided to end her life by throwing herself into the sea.

When she went down into the water, a handsome young sailor noticed her tears and took pity on her.

"Look, you've got a lot to live for," he said. "I'm off to America in the morning and if you like I can stow you away on my ship. I'll take good care of you and bring you food every day."

Moving closer, he slipped his arm around her shoulder and added: "I'll keep you happy and you'll keep me happy."

The girl nodded. After all, what did she have to lose?

That night, the sailor brought her aboard and hid her in a lifeboat. From then on, every night he brought her three sandwiches and a piece of fruit and they made passionate love until dawn.

Three weeks later during a routine search, the captain discovered her.

"What are you doing here," the captain asked.

"I have an arrangement with one of the sailors," she said. "He's taking me to America, and he's feeding me."

"What are you doing for him," said the captain.

"He's doing me," said the girl.

"He certainly is," replied the captain. "This is the Stranraer to Larne ferry!"

165

I DECIDED to take a day off from work and go golfing. I was on the fourth tee when I discovered a small frog. I paid it no attention until I heard: "Ribbit. Nine iron."

That's curious, I thought, but decided to trust the frog. I pulled out a nine iron, and sunk a hole-in-one. Amazing! So I picked up the frog and headed to the fifth hole. I asked the frog what club to used and it said: "Ribbit. Three wood."

I used that club and sunk another hole-in-one! I continued an amazing round of golf. At the end, I asked the frog where we should go next. It answered: "Ribbit. Vegas."

So we went to Las Vegas and I asked the frog what we should do first.

"Ribbit. Roulette."

So we went up to the roulette table and I asked the frog how much I should wager.

"Ribbit. Three thousand dollars."

It was a lot of money, but I ponied up anyway. Needless to say, I won big! I took my earnings and got the best room in the hotel. Once we were up there, I asked the frog if there was anything I could do to repay it.

"Ribbit. Kiss me."

I thought, what the hell, it's just a frog. So I kissed the frog, and it turned into a 15-year-old girl.

That's how she ended up in my room, and if I'm lying, my name is not William Jefferson Clinton.

WHY do farts smell so bad?
So that the deaf can enjoy them too.

WHAT'S the best position to make ugly babies?
Ask your parents.

TWO couples are playing cards. John accidentally drops some cards on the floor. When he bends down under the table to pick them up, he notices that Bill's wife isn't wearing any underwear!

Shocked by this, John hits his head on the table and emerges red-faced. Later, John goes to the kitchen to get some refreshments. Bill's wife follows him and asks: "Did you see anything that you liked under there?"

John admits that, well, yes, he did.

She says: "You can have it, but it will cost you £100."

After a minute or two, John indicates that he is interested. She tells him that since Bill works on Friday afternoons he should come to her house at two o'clock on that day.

Friday comes and John goes to her house at two o'clock. After paying her £100 they go to the bedroom and have sex. Then John leaves. Bill comes home about six and asks his wife: "Did John come by this afternoon?"

Hesitantly, she replies: "Yes, he did stop by for a few minutes."

Next Bill asks: "Did he give you £100?"

She thinks: "Oh hell, he knows!" Finally she says: "Well, yes... He did give me £100."

"Good," Bill says. "John came by the office this morning and borrowed £100 from me. He said that he would stop by our house on his way home to pay me back."

167

THREE couples go to see the minister to ask how to become members of his church. The minister said that they would have to go without sex for two weeks and then come back and tell him how it went.

The first couple was retired, the second couple was middle-aged and the final couple was newly wed.

Two weeks went by, and the couples returned to the church. The retired couple said it was no problem at all. The middle-aged couple said it was tough for the first week, but after that, it was no problem.

The newly-weds said it was fine until she dropped the can of paint.

"Can of paint," exclaimed the minister.

"Aye," said the man. "She dropped the can and when she bent over to pick it up I had to have her right there and then. Lust took over."

The minister just shook his head and said that they were not welcome in his church.

"That's okay," said the man. "We're not welcome in B&Q either."

A COUPLE goes to an art gallery. They find a picture of a naked women with only her privates covered with leaves. The wife doesn't like it and moves on but the huband keeps looking. The wife asks: "What are you waiting for?" The husband replies: "Autumn."

A LITTLE kid goes on to a bus, sits right behind the driver and starts yelling: "If my dad was a bull and my mum a cow I'd be a little bull."

The driver starts getting annoyed at the noisy kid, who continues with: "If my dad was an elephant and my mum a girl elephant I would be a little elephant."

The kid goes on with several animals until the bus driver gets really angry and yells: "What if your dad was gay and your mom was a prostitute?"

The kid smiles and says: "I would be a bus driver!"

SEX is like a bank account. You put it in, you take it out, you lose interest.

ED and Ted are standing at the urinals in a public toilet, when Ed glances down and notices that Ted's manhood is twisted like a corkscrew.

"I've never seen one like that before," he says.

"Like what," Ted answers.

"All twisted like a pig's tail."

"Well, what's yours like," asks Ted.

"Straight, like normal."

"I thought mine was normal until I saw yours," Ted says.

Ed finishes what he was doing and gives his old boy a shake prior to putting it back in his trousers.

"What did you do that for," Ted asks.

"Shaking off the excess drops," Ed says. "Like normal."

"Damn," Ted says. "All these years I've been wringing it."

A KNIGHT marches off to join the Crusades. He decides to lock his wife in a chastity belt while he is gone and gives the key to his best friend. He tells him: "If I'm not back within four years, unlock my wife and set her free to live a normal life."

So, the husband leaves on horseback but about a half hour later, he sees a cloud of dust behind him. He waits and sees his best friend galloping up.

"What's wrong," he asks.

"You gave me the wrong key!"

TWO wee boys go into a supermarket. One is nine and the other is four. The nine-year-old grabs a box of tampons from the shelf and carries it to the check-out.

The shop assistant says: "Oh, these must be for your mummy?"

The nine-year-old replies: "No, not for my mum." Without thinking, the cashier replies: "Well, they must be for your sister then?"

The nine-year-old says: "Nope, not for my sister either."

The cashier had now become curious.

"Oh. If they're not for your mummy or sister, then who are they for?""

The nine-year old says: "They're for my four-year-old brother."

The cashier is surprised but the nine-year-old explains:

"Well, they say on television that if you wear one of these, you can swim and ride a bike – and my little brother can't do either of those things."

DID you hear about the cannibal who spent so long in the pub that he was late for dinner? *His wife gave him the cold shoulder!*

A DRIVER swerved to avoid hitting a rabbit in the middle of the road, but unfortunately it jumped in front of the car and was hit.

Being a sensitive man, as well as an animal lover, he pulled over to the side of the road, and got out to see what had become of the rabbit. Much to his dismay, the rabbit was dead.

The driver felt so awful, he began to cry. A woman saw the man crying at the side of the road and pulled over. She stepped out of her car and asked the man what was wrong.

"I feel terrible," he explained. "I accidentally hit this rabbit and killed it."

The woman told the man not to worry. She knew what to do. She went into the boot of her car, and pulled out a spray can. She walked over to the limp, dead rabbit, and sprayed the contents of the can onto it.

Miraculously the rabbit came to life, jumped up and hopped down the road.

The man was astonished. He couldn't think what substance could be in the woman's spray can.

He asked: "What is in your spray can? What did you spray on that rabbit?"

The woman turned the can around so that the man could read the label. It said: "Hair spray. Restores life to dead hair."

THERE was this shepherd who had this whole flock of sheep. He wanted to get the sheep pregnant so that he could increase his stock but he was too poor to buy a ram. So, he thought, the only thing he could do was to get the sheep pregnant himself.

One morning the man loaded up all the sheep into his truck and drove them over to a barn where nobody could see him.

He serviced each sheep in turn and then loaded them back on to the truck and brought them back to the pasture near his house. He went to bed that night after a long day's work.

The next morning he woke up, and looked out the bedroom window expecting all the sheep to be laying down on their sides, because that is what the sheep do when they are pregnant. But, all the sheep were still standing.

The guy is surprised and a little disappointed, but he gets up, loads the sheep back into the truck, takes them to the barn and tries to get them impregnated.

He wakes up the next morning and looks out the window and sees that the sheep are all standing up. So, he loads them in the truck, takes them in the barn and does them all, yet again.

The next morning, he is so exhausted by his work, he asks his wife to look out the window and look at the sheep. She does this and he asks her if they are laying down on their sides.

She says: "No, they are all in the truck, and one is honking the horn!"

A WOMAN met a man at a club and went back to his
  place for sex. Afterward, she said: "You must be a
  good dentist."
He replied: "How did you know I'm a dentist."
She said: "I didn't feel a thing."

A PRIMARY school class had a homework assignment to
  find out about something exciting and relate it to the
  class the next day.
When the time came to present what they'd found, the
  first little boy walked up to the front of the class made
  a small white dot on the blackboard then sat back
  down. Puzzled, the teacher asked him just what it was.
"It's a period," said the little boy.
"Well, I can see that," said the teacher. "But what is so
  exciting about a period?"
"Don't know, miss,'" said the little boy. "But this morning
  my sister was missing one, daddy had a heart attack,
  mummy fainted and the man next door shot himself."

A GUY is on a date with this girl, so he takes her to
  Lover's Lane. When they get up there, she say: "I
  have to be honest with you, I'm a hooker."
The guy thinks about this and eventually agrees to
  pay her £25.
So they start having sex. After they finish, the man
  says: "Now I have to be honest with you. I'm a taxi
  driver and it'll cost you £25 for me to drive you
  back into town."

THREE men are in a doctor's surgery. One is a drunk, one's a heavy smoker and the third is gay.

The doctor tells each of them that, if they induldge in their bad habit one more time, they will die.

Outside they pass a bar. The drunk says: "I don't care if I die, I need a drink."

He goes into the bar, takes a drink and, sure enough, he drops dead.

The smoker and the gay guy continue walking along.

Then the smoker spots a lit cigarette on the pavement.

The gay guy looks over and says: "If you bend down to pick that up, we're both dead."

A DUCK walks into a bar and asks: "Got any grapes?"

The barman tells the ducks that the bar doesn't serve grapes. The duck thanks him and leaves.

The next day, the duck returns and says: "Got any grapes?"

Again, the barman tells him that they do not serve grapes, never have served grapes and, furthermore, never will serve grapes. The duck, a little ruffled, thanks him and leaves.

Next day, the duck returns, but before he can say anything, the barman yells: "Listen, duck! This is a pub! We do not serve grapes! If you ever ask for grapes again, I will nail your stupid duck beak to the bar!"

The duck is silent for a moment, and then asks: "Got any nails?"

Confused, the barman says no.

"Good," says the duck. "Got any grapes?"

WHAT do you give a deer
with an upset stomach?
Elk-a-seltzer.

THIS elephant is walking through the jungle when she
gets a thorn in her foot. The further she walks, the
sorer it gets. After a while she starts to limp.

An ant walks up and asks: "Hey, what's the matter?"

The elephant answers: "I've got this thorn in my foot
and I would do anything to get it out."

The ant says: "Anything? Would you let me make love to
you?"

The elephant thinks about it for a minute and decides
what the heck. How bad can an ant be? So she agrees.

The ant starts pulling on the thorn and sure enough, he
gets it out. True to her word, the elephant lies down on
her side and moves her tail out of the way. The ant
crawls up and starts making sweet love to her.

A monkey is up in a tree watching this. He can't quite
believe his eyes. He starts laughing and rolling around
in the tree. Then he knocks a coconut out of the tree
that crashes down and hits the elephant right between
the ears.

The elephant moans loudly from the hit:
"Awwooooohhhhh!"

The ant yells at the top of his voice: "Take it all darling,
take it all!"

WHERE do you find a
no-legged dog?
Right where you left him!

THREE turtles, Joe, Gerry, and Ray, go on a picnic. Joe packs the picnic basket with biscuits, bottles of coke and sandwiches. Trouble is, the picnic site is ten miles away, so the turtles take ten days to get there.

By the time they arrive, everyone is exhausted. Joe begins to unpack. He takes out the bottles and says: "Alright, Gerry, gimme the bottle opener."

"I didn't bring the bottle opener," Gerry says. "I thought you packed it."

Joe turns to Ray: "Do you have the bottle opener?"

Ray doesn't have it, so the turtles are stuck ten miles away from home without anything to drink.

Joe and Gerry beg Ray to turn back home and retrieve it, but Ray flatly refuses, knowing that they'll have eaten everything by the time he gets back.

After about two hours, the turtles manage to convince Ray to go, swearing that they won't touch the food. So, Ray sets off down the road, slow and steady. Three weeks pass, but no Ray. Joe and Gerry are hungry and puzzled, but a promise is a promise.

Another day passes and still there is no sign of Ray, but a promise is a promise.

After three more days without Ray in sight, Gerry starts getting restless. "I need food," he cries.

"No," Joe retorts. "We promised."

Five more days pass. By now Joe and Gerry are desperate.

So the two turtles weakly lift the lid of the picnic basket, take out a sandwich each, and open their mouths to eat.

Then, right at that instant, Ray pops out from behind a rock, and shouts: "I knew it! I'm not blooming going."

Books available from our collection:

You are my Larsson: The Henrik Larsson Story	£5.95
The Martin O'Neill Story	£5.95
The 2002 Prize Crossword Book	£4.99
The Billy Sloan Rock and Pop Quiz Book	£4.99
The Jim Traynor/Hugh Keevins Sports Quiz Book	£4.99
The Joe Punter Racing Guide	£4.99
The Tam Cowan Joke Book	£4.99
VIDEO: Lubo – A Gift From God	£14.99

All these books are available at your local bookshop or newsagent, or can be ordered direct form the publisher. Indicate the number of copies required and fill in the form below.

Send to: *First Press Publishing,*
Daily Record and Sunday Mail,
1 Central Quay,
Glasgow, G3 8DA

or phone: **0141 309 1425** quoting title, author and credit or debit card number.

or fax: **0141 309 3304**, quoting title, author and credit or debit card number.

or email: **orders@first-press.co.uk**

Enclose a remittance* to the value of the cover price plus 75p per book for postage and packing. European customers allow £1.50 per book for post and packing.

* Payment may be made in sterling by UK personal cheque, Eurocheque, postal order, sterling draft or international money order, made payable to First Press Publishing.

Alternatively by Visa/Mastercard/Debit Card Card No.

Expiry Date ☐☐☐☐   Valid From Date ☐☐☐☐   Issue Number ☐

Signature: _____

Applicable only in the UK and BFPO addresses.

While every effort is made to keep prices low, it is sometimes necessary to increase prices at short notice. First Press Publishing reserve the right to show on covers and charges new retail prices which may differ form those advertised in the text or elsewhere.

NAME AND ADDRESS (IN BLOCK CAPITALS PLEASE)

Name _____

Address _____

_____

_____ Postcode_____

First Press will use your information for administration and analysis. We may share it with carefully selected third parties. We, or they, may send you details of goods and services. The information may be provided by letter, telephone or other.
If you do not want your details to be shared please tick this box.   ☐